THE DISAPPEARING NINTH LEGION

A POPULAR HISTORY

(Loosely based on: 'The Ninth Legion, Its History And Mysterious Disappearance', John Aspin Publications, 1997.)

THE DISAPPEARING NINTH LEGION

A POPULAR HISTORY

(Loosely based on: 'The Ninth Legion, Its History And
Mysterious Disappearance', John Aspin Publications, 1997.)

MARK OLLY

WITH JOHN ASPIN

BOOKS

Winchester, UK
Washington, USA

First published by O-Books, 2011
O-Books is an imprint of John Hunt Publishing Ltd., Laurel House, Station Approach,
Alresford, Hants, SO24 9JH, UK
office1@o-books.net
www.o-books.com

For distributor details and how to order please visit the 'Ordering' section on our website.

Text copyright: Mark Olly and John Aspin 2010

ISBN: 978 1 84694 559 5

A CIP catalogue record for this book is available from the British Library.

Design: Stuart Davies

Printed in the UK by CPI Antony Rowe
Printed in the USA by Offset Paperback Mfrs, Inc

We operate a distinctive and ethical publishing philosophy in all
areas of our business, from our global network of authors to
production and worldwide distribution.

CONTENTS

Mark Olly would like to dedicate this book to Andrea Thomason,
"My first love, lost for many years but now found."

John Aspin would like to dedicate this book to his late mother
Winnefred Mary Aspin,
1917 to 2009.

This book constitutes a modern adaptation of primarily original Roman source material found in Tacitus' *'Annals Of Imperial Rome'*, Julius Caesar's *'Gallic Wars'* & *'Conquest Of Gaul'*, Fronto's *'Letters'*, and a host of antiquarian & archaeological publications covering 300 years of research not readily available to today's public.

Thanks/Dedications Etc.

Mark Olly received much help in the preparation of this work & would like to express his gratitude to the following for their assistance: John Aspin, Andrea Thomason for getting this project moving again, Mum & Dad for inspiration, Helen Maria Carr for critically reviewing the first draft, Phil Hirst & all the 'Lost Treasures'/'Britain's Lost Mega Fortress' TV programs' Roman advisers, many archaeologists (you know who you are!) & Roman re-enactors in York & Chester, without whose enthusiasm & encouragement this book would never have been completed.

John Aspin received much help in the preparation of this work & would like to express his gratitude to the following for their assistance: Mark Olly, Graham Browne, Dr James Cantlie, Karen Svanso & Tracy Fitzsimons for illustrations, Alison Player, Nigel Player, Nike French, Victoria Aspin, York Library, Glossop Library, Carlisle Museum. John Aspin would also like to acknowledge the help & encouragement he had from the late Dr Derryck Ward, & also the invaluable help from Dr Patrick Ottaway of the York Archaeological Trust who continue the work to this day.

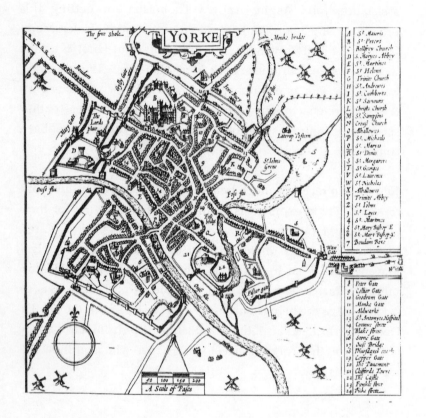

John Speed's Map Of Surviving Roman & Medieval York 1611

I

Introduction - The Golden Slipper

A summer shower was pouring from the heavens when I met John outside the 'Golden Slipper' in York, a tiny pub on the edge of The Shambles built in the 15th and 16th centuries, and given a somewhat 'quirky' brick façade in the industrial enthusiasm of the 19th century.

The earliest account of the place reads: *"John Armstrong was returning from having a few at the sign of The Slipper in Goodramgate"* when William Brown had *"severely beaten and thrown him into the river until he was stiff and stagnated with cold."*

That's how I felt as we shook the water from our coats and settled in for lunch and *'a few'* of our own. At least I wasn't about to be hanged on Baille Hill for robbery like William Brown had been, as reported in the York Gazette of 17th March 1821! As always discussion turned to the fact that no popular book had yet been written about the foundation of York city by the Roman Ninth Legion.

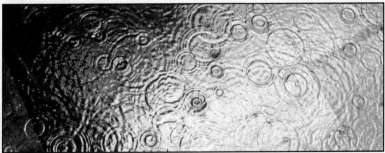

I mused:*"I hate Romans! The world we now live in is dominated by Roman ways and Roman thoughts, frequently without any regard for those cultures they conquered and absorbed into the 'Empire'. I'm a big fan of those cultures, the Celts. So why should I write a book devoted to some of the greatest battles, conquests, and political issues to occur in over a thousand years of Roman history?"*

John was persuasive: *"I love a good mystery, don't you? It was this aspect, the disappearance of an entire Legion apparently somewhere in the UK, that first caught my attention years ago. Then to find that no popular history of this Legion and these events had ever been written beyond the pages of fiction came as a bit of a shock!"*

John won his argument and here it is, *'**The Disappearing Ninth Legion, A Popular History**'*, historic research and concept by John Aspin, written and photographed by myself, Mark Olly.

Whether you are a fan of the Romans or not, you will find this fast-paced account a gripping historic 'whodunnit' which may never have a satisfactory resolution – unless, one day, you meet a bedraggled Legion of defeated soldiers trudging through the mists on some forgotten moorland road, or the ghost of a skin-cloaked standard bearer still desperately searching for his missing golden eagle!

Mark Olly (Summer 2010 AD).

York: Ebur, Eburacum (*Antonian Itinerary* C.380 AD) / Eboracensis, Euborica, Eoforwic (*Old English Chronicles* C.780 AD) / Caer Ebrauc, Eferwic, Eurvich (*Domesday* 1086 AD & *Layam* 1205 AD).

All we know of the area around York before the arrival of the Romans is a collection of small Iron Age farmsteads which can be seen surrounding the city on aerial photographs and satellite images, but not yet ever found within the city. The ancient Roman historian Ptolemy mentions *'Eborakon'* as one of the settlements of the Brigantes, a tribe which occupied the whole of Northern England before and throughout the Roman occupation and the probable owners of the local farmsteads.

The name is said to originate from the Irish-Gaelic *'ebrach'*, meaning *'muddy'* or *'a marsh'* ending in *'ach'* meaning *'place of'*. The Angles may have taken it to be 'town, dwelling (*'wic'*) on the river (*'Ure'*)' and it is this *'Eure'* which looks like *'iubhar/ibar'* which has led to *'a yew'* and the interpretation *'the place of the yews'*.

Given that this could equate to a grove of yew trees located in a marsh, it has been said that the Romans took over a Druid sacred site and retained its original name as they had done elsewhere.

Was it this act that brought down the original curse on the 'Unlucky Ninth'?

Minerva - Roman Goddess Of Wisdom And Drama In The Shambles

"Nature itself has removed Britain beyond the power and jurisdiction of the gods of Rome... to war beyond the bounds of nature is not courage, but impiety."
Emperor Caligula (37 AD – 41 AD)

II

MARCHING INTO ETERNITY

Roman legends date the founding of Rome to 753 BC. The city was built on a hilly site about twenty miles from the coast in order to defend it from the frequent raids by Greek and Phoenician ships. The first buildings were clustered around Palatine Hill, where later emperors of Imperial Rome built huge palaces, and the first ruler was a Latin Chieftain called Romulus. Romulus initiated the first citizen army who fought on foot and would probably have looked more like ancient Greek soldiers (hoplites) than the popular image of Roman Legionaries.

The early army used a long slashing sword, a round shield and bronze helmets, with only the well-off wearing armour consisting of a breast plate of beaten bronze in various designs. Other weapons included spears, javelins, battle axes and daggers. Later the army was formed into 'centuries' of 80 to 100 men with a full army having as many as 50 'centurions' in it, split into various classes:

I)   Heavy Spearmen,
II) Medium Spearmen,
III) Light Spearmen,
IV) Javelineers, Archers, Slingers,
V)   Veterans (Home Guard)

It was to take almost 600 years for Rome to bring all Italy under her control and to encompass their neighbours the Etruscans and Samnites, but Rome held on to her states, unlike the constantly warring Greeks. Within two hundred years of Italy becoming united, Rome had built her Empire with the best infantry in the world comprised of her citizens. Each citizen who joined the army was supplied by the state. The uniform of the Legionary, weapons, armour, short-sleeved or long-sleeved cold weather tunic, studded sandals, and other kit, were deducted from their pay.

By the time the Ninth Legion was formed in the first century BC, the Roman Army had become divided into units of 4,800 men called 'Legions', each divided into 'Cohorts' of 480 men, divided again into three 'Maniples' of 160 men, and then again into two 'Centuries' of 80 men, and finally into 10 'Contubernia' of eight men each.

Each Legion also had a small detachment of cavalry of around 120 men. Only in later times did the 'Legion' become 6,000 men, the 'Cohort' 600 men and the 'Century' the familiar 100 men.

Upon Emperor Claudius' suggestion that they should invade Britain in 43 AD, the Roman Legions mutinied saying: *"We will march anywhere in the world but not out of it."* Nevertheless, out of it they were to march, beyond the jurisdiction of their gods, beyond the assistance of Imperial Rome, indeed beyond the bounds of nature itself! In 43 AD they came as a permanent invasion force to the shores of Britain.

The Ninth 'Hispana' (or 'Spanish Legion', so called from earlier campaigns) came from Pannonia in Central Europe with Claudius in 43 AD and was established at Lincoln by 47 AD. It was engaged in campaigns against the Brigantes in 51 and 52 AD under the command of Caesius Nasica, and was cut up by rebels during Boudicca's revolt in 60 to 61 AD while under Petillius Cerialis.

By 70 AD they were upon the gates of the north, they were beyond the sacred goddess river Belisama (Mersey) and the central homelands of the Druids. They had unwisely entered 'Eburacon', the 'Place of the Yews', and left their own world far behind – possibly for eternity. The Ninth Legion arrived in York in 71 AD when Cerialis was Governor and was last heard of there between 107 and 108 AD. And there begins the mystery.

It is thought that, some time between the years 117 and 120 AD, the Ninth Legion marched out towards the north to deal with the tribes in Caledonia (Scotland) who had, for some time, caused much trouble with uprisings against the Roman occupation of their lands. Most of the Ninth Legion, along with auxiliary infantry and cavalry, with civilian support, a force that may have totalled 10,000 men, were never heard of again. The entire force just disappeared. Not one soldier returned and no remains were ever found. Or so the legend goes!

However, recent evidence suggests that the Ninth Legion was still in existence well after 120 AD, and that it may have been transferred to Nijmegen soon after this date – or was it those few soldiers who were left behind to defend Eboracum who were sent there to regroup? Recent evidence also suggests the Legion was later transferred to the east and may well have been the one destroyed in the early part of the war against the Parthians in 161 AD. The total loss of the Ninth Legion has become one of the greatest unsolved military mysteries of all time.

In the undercroft of the Minster lie the remains of the Roman 'principia' or military headquarters, from which ran the 'Via Decumana', a north-easterly highway through the Forest of Galtres. The highway itself can still be found, along with the gritstone base of a Roman column, in the cellars of the Treasurer's House, and it is here that our story begins.

The Treasurer's House York

III

The Plumber's Apprentice

In 1953 the Treasurer's House was in the process of modernization and Harry Martindale was an apprentice plumber employed to help fit the new central heating system down in the cellars. He was halfway up a short ladder when he thought he heard a single blast from a distant horn through the thick cellar walls. As he was underground he dismissed the noise until it sounded again a little louder and a little closer, totally tuneless and consisting of a single blast. This was repeated several times, each time louder and closer, until a figure emerged from the solid stone wall. Its head was in line with Harry's waist and wore a shining helmet.

Harry fell from the ladder and scrambled into a corner from where he realized that the figure was that of a dejected Roman soldier with his head bowed. The figure trudged through the room and disappeared through the opposite wall. He was immediately followed by another soldier sat astride a large, shaggy carthorse, leading an equally dejected troop of between 12 and 20 foot soldiers tramping side by side. They also crossed the room at an angle and vanished into the opposite wall!

Harry froze throughout his ordeal, afraid that any movement might alert the soldiers to his presence, but as soon as they were gone he bolted for the safety of the rooms above where he was found collapsed at the top of the cellar steps by the curator of the Treasurer's House. The curator simply commented, *"You look*

as though you have just seen the Roman ghosts!"

The most important aspects of this incident were the eye-witness accounts given by Harry Martindale of what he had seen. There was nothing smart about their appearance. They wore handmade garments of green cloth in various shades and were in great need of a wash and a shave, and it was unusual to see ghosts in colour. They were all wearing the same basic type of helmet which had fine plumes of 'feathers' bristling from the top and continuing down the back, to hang at the neck. Plumes of this type were usually made of stiffened horse hair. Each carried a short-bladed sword on their right side, spears which they dragged, and at least one had a round, green shield without a device.

Harry also noticed that they were all very short, probably on account of their lower legs being below floor level until they reached the centre of the room. Here Harry noted their lower

legs on an area of the 'Via Decumana' Roman road recently unearthed by archaeologists 18 inches below the cellar floor. The only sound Harry could remember was the noise of the horses' hooves and low murmurs which began as they drew near the centre of the room but did not appear to issue from the soldiers themselves!

Some time later Harry Martindale was questioned and his account tested by scholars and historians. They were impressed by his description of the Roman soldiers, and especially the only recently discovered 'round shields', which they felt dated to the later part of the first century AD. They deduced that Harry Martindale had seen the final remains of the defeated Ninth Legion returning to a shocked Roman city of Eboracum between the years 108 AD and 122 AD.

IV

THE 'PLACE OF THE YEWS'

In 71 AD the Romans arrived, displaced the local Brigantes, Parisi and Druids, and established a town called 'Eboracum', 'The Place of the Yews', now known as York.

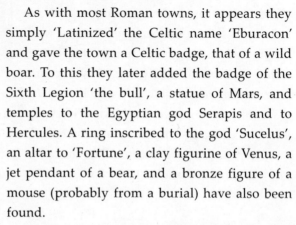

As with most Roman towns, it appears they simply 'Latinized' the Celtic name 'Eburacon' and gave the town a Celtic badge, that of a wild boar. To this they later added the badge of the Sixth Legion 'the bull', a statue of Mars, and temples to the Egyptian god Serapis and to Hercules. A ring inscribed to the god 'Sucelus', an altar to 'Fortune', a clay figurine of Venus, a jet pendant of a bear, and a bronze figure of a mouse (probably from a burial) have also been found.

Roman York occupied about 50 acres and housed a mighty fighting force of 6,000 heavy infantry in preparation for the great push north which, in reality, never really came. Notwithstanding, it remained a major headquarters for the Roman army in northern Britain for over 300 years. In an empire based on military might the strength of the army gave York considerable importance to the extent that it was visited by the military leaders of Rome including the emperors themselves.

York must have had accommodation and amenities fit for these emperors, their empresses, and the associated court; evidence of this is the three years from 208 AD to 211 AD where surviving records show that Emperor Severus governed Britain, and directed campaigns from York, and then remained there until his death.

Two emperors died in Britain, both in York: Septimius Severus in 221 AD and Constantius I (Chlorus) in 306 AD. Upon the death of Constantius his son, Constantine, was proclaimed by the legionaries as his successor in York starting a career which led to him to become Constantine 'The Great', the Emperor credited with 'legalizing' Christianity across the Roman Empire. A magnificent stone head of Constantine was found in Stonegate York at some point before 1823, a fitting memorial to this great leader.

Historians speak of a palace at York, and a great city did

indeed grow up next to the fortress, holding the highest possible status, that of 'Colonia', which gave it a large measure of self-government. By the third century York had become the capital of 'Lower Britain', one of the two 'provinces' into which the

Romans had divided Britain. By the fourth century it remained a provincial capital when Britain was divided into four provinces in the 'prefecture of the Gauls'. In 314 AD three British bishops attended the Christian Council at Arles in France and one of these came from York.

The site is typical of a legionary fortress, set on a ridge of high ground in the junction of a tidal river (Ouse) and a tributary (Foss) which could provide a harbour. The fortress was the usual rectangular 'playing card' plan with rounded corners and a long axis orientated north-east to south-west.

The main gate, or *'porta praetoria'*, was central to the south-west side which faced the river Ouse and a bridge. The site of this gate is now in St Helen's Square – aptly named after the wife of Constantine The Great. Stonegate, the street leading from this square towards the Minster, is mostly on the line of the Roman *'via principalis'* which linked the gates on the north-west and south-east sides. The *'portae principales'* links the sites along Bootham Bar and King's Square, and a rear gate, the *'porta decumana'*, which was central on the north-east side, lies under the Medieval rampart. Four gates linked by four principal internal roads.

York Minster inside the Roman fort.

York Minster now occupies the site of the Roman headquarters buildings, the 'principia', and a rear courtyard once housed a great hall based on the Roman structure still standing and recorded as being larger than the Minster nave at that time. Sadly, like so much of Roman York, this building has long been consigned to the pages of history; however, the Minster still houses considerable Roman remains on display in its Undercroft Museum, and a massive column found in 1969 has been re-erected opposite the south door.

ROMAN COLUMN

THIS ROMAN COLUMN ONCE STOOD WITHIN THE GREAT HALL OF THE HEADQUARTERS BUILDING OF THE FORTRESS OF THE SIXTH LEGION (WHOSE EMBLEM WAS A BULL) IN THE FOURTH CENTURY A.D. IT WAS FOUND IN 1969 DURING THE EXCAVATION OF THE SOUTH TRANSEPT OF THE MINSTER. LYING WHERE IT HAD COLLAPSED. IT WAS GIVEN BY THE DEAN & CHAPTER TO THE YORK CIVIC TRUST, WHO IN 1971 ERECTED IT ON THIS SITE TO MARK THE 1900TH ANNIVERSARY OF THE FOUNDATION OF THE CITY BY THE ROMANS IN A.D. 71.

Other buildings within the fortress included the Commander's house, officers' quarters, barrack blocks, a hospital, stores and baths, but few of these remain on view. Excavations down the years have revealed details of the rampart walls and ditches, a few barrack blocks, part of the Tribune's house, and a late baths building, the cold plunge pool of which is preserved under the 'Roman Bath' inn on St Sampson's Square.

Of interest to the occupation period of the Ninth Legion are the initial defences.

Once the site was cleared in 71 AD the ramparts of the first fortress were rapidly constructed from local materials as the expeditionary force were clearly in hostile territory. Green boughs were lopped and trimmed to be laid as foundations on to which earth dug from a surrounding ditch was piled into a bank faced with turfs.

Around 80 AD during Agricola's governorship, a foundation

of heavy beams of seasoned wood were laid over the now spread remains of the first rampart. A new earth bank was then piled on top of this, revetted with turf, and surmounted by a timber palisade and heavy towers inside a double ditch. Buildings inside the fort were timber-framed with wattle and daub plaster infill and some great cooking ovens were sited well away from buildings at the back of the rampart, the base of one which can still be seen near the Multangular Tower.

Around 107 AD to 108 AD an inscription was carved recording the building of the new south-east gate in stone under the Emperor Trajan, in what is now King's Square, by the Ninth Legion. This came to light in 1854 and supports evidence from other parts of the fortress which shows that the inner ditch was filled in with the old turf facing as it was replaced with a stone wall and stone towers. Rome was here to stay – or so the Romans thought, as this is the last actual act recorded by the Ninth Legion.

In the late second or early third century the whole of the defences were rebuilt again on securer foundations and it is to this date that the fortress wall which emerges from below the Medieval wall at the east corner belongs. Elsewhere the fortress was finally rebuilt around 300 AD with two mighty multangular towers and six others in between, probably in honour of its position in the Romano-British scheme of things. Much internal work was also undertaken during the Constantinian period.

It is known that the Colonia was, in turn,

surrounded by burial grounds along the principle highways, and it is from these areas to the south that we get the statue of Mars (found in 1880) and a coffin containing the remains of 'Julia Victoriana', finds that bring us closer to the actual people who occupied the fortress in the days of the Ninth Legion. The Standard-Bearer *'L. Duccius Rufinus'* records on his tombstone that he was born in Vienne in Gaul, came to York to serve in the Ninth Legion, and died at the age of 28. He still stands proud, carved on his tombstone with his standard in his right hand, one of a number of tombstones and dedications to survive. So what were these soldiers like?

V

WHAT WAS A 'LEGION'?

When the Ninth Legion was first formed, the Legionary wore a helmet of Greek origin, chain mail armour known as 'lorica hamata' and carried a short 'gladius' sword with a 53 centimetre long double-edged blade, bone grip and bronze pommel, worn on the right. His shield was a curved oval about 1.6 metres high, made from laminated wood covered in leather and painted with the Legion's colours which, in the case of the Ninth Legion, are thought to have been green. The Legionary also carried a short dagger called a 'pugio' on his left side which would have acted as a multi-purpose knife for eating and working, as well as for use in close combat or if shields became interlocked.

He could carry a pickaxe called a *'dolabra'*, an entrenching tool and a turf cutter. He would also often have a *'pilum'* javelin with a 1.52 metre wooden shaft attached to a metal shaft with a small spearhead at the end.

Julius Caesar modified this to include an untempered area behind the point which caused it to bend after being thrown so it could not be thrown back by the British. The metal part could then be replaced later after use.

As well as carrying equipment for war and setting up camp, his kit also included rations for at least three days carried in a net, a stone for grinding grain, bronze cooking pot and pan, a bag with his cloak, spare underwear, a first aid kit, shaving kit and a 'Y' shaped carrying pole which brought the weight of his gear to between 38 and 40 kilos.

The equipment of the Ninth Legion gradually changed during its existence. Mail armour continued to be used by Legionaries but a new type called *'Lorica Segmentata'* came into use in Tiberius' reign between 14 AD and 37 AD. This plate armour was a lot stronger than chain mail, which could be torn open by hooked axes. The reason for the change given by military historians was the great defeat of the Governor Varus and three Legions in the Teutoburg Forest in 9 AD where the chain mail uniform failed to give enough protection to the Roman foot soldiers.

The helmet changed to give greater protection to the back of the head like the Gallic versions of the day, and the shield became rectangular and curved. The dagger was dropped altogether. To some extent the Ninth Legion would also have been modernized by Emperor Claudius in readiness for the invasion of Britain in 43 AD, but they may have retained some of the old style equipment such as the oval shield and the dagger. By their disappearance in the early second century circular shields were back in fashion.

There is no doubt that the Ninth Legion had a detachment of 'Alae' (meaning 'Wings'), about 120 cavalrymen who would have been employed as scouts and dispatch riders and increased in number during significant campaigns. The Romans were excellent foot soldiers but mediocre horsemen hence the name 'Wings', as the cavalry were almost always used on the flanks of the famous Roman infantry. Many foreign mercenaries were brought in as cavalry until efforts were made to correct this in the 3rd, 4th and 5th centuries, long after the Ninth Legion had disappeared.

The Ninth Legion also had 'Auxiliaries' divided into 'Cohorts' under the command of 'Prefects' (Officers), and frequently made up of soldiers from the same tribe or nation allied to Rome for particular campaigns or by certain Chieftains. Later on their equipment was also standardized and they were used more and more along the frontiers taking pressure off the Legions. Auxiliary forts can be found all over the frontiers of the Roman Empire, and Auxiliaries would have marched out of York with the Ninth Legion on its fateful last journey north.

The Legion and its Auxiliary units were commanded by a *'Legatus'* who usually held his position for about three years. Under him were six military *'Tribunes'* of which at least one would be a young man of high birth intended for a Senatorial career. He would serve two or three years then, at the age of 25, would enter the Senate in Rome as a *'Quester'*. His main job was to learn the art of 'Generalship' so that he could qualify in 10 to 15 years for *'Legateship'* of a Legion. The other five tribunes were men over the age of 30 who had served as Prefects or Auxiliary Cohorts but hoped to go on further in command of other units such as the Cavalry.

They were employed as Staff Officers at the Legionary Headquarters but could find themselves occasionally in command of detachments during a campaign.

When the Ninth Legion left Eboracum a senior tribune may well have been left in charge of the remaining garrison holding the city. The senior professional officer at the Legion Headquarters was the *'Camp Prefect'* who was responsible for the internal organization, equipment, general stores and training schedule for the soldiers. He would have had at least 25 years of service behind him.

The backbone of the Ninth Legion would, without any doubt, have been the *'Centurions'*, called by the Auxiliaries *'Decurions'*,

and in charge of a 'Century' of men. Each Legion had 60 Centurions, the majority of which had risen from the ranks of ordinary soldiers. The *'Senior Centurion'* served in the First Cohort and, commanding the First Century, was the *'Chief Centurion'* who was a man of at least 45 years of age.

Under him came the *'Princeps'* who were responsible for the office work of their Legion. The Junior Officer in each Century was known as the *'Tesseranus'* responsible for the watch word of the camp and organizing fatigue parties. In addition to him, each

Legion had a Standard Bearer known as the *'Aquilfer'* to carry the Imperial Eagle, another known as the *'Imaginifer'* to carry the standard depicting the Emperor and the *'Signifer'* who carried the standard of the Century's Emblem; in the case of the Ninth Legion this may have been a boar or, like the Sixth Legion (also based at York), a bull.

Other specialist craftsmen could be found accompanying a Legion. The *'Architectus'* was the Master Builder with his *'Mensor'* or Surveyor and his *'Hydzaulazious'* responsible for sanitation and water supply. Every Legion had priests and soothsayers and a *'Medicus Ordinarius'* or Medical Officer.

A Legion familiar with conflict would also have war machines, many of which the Romans had copied from the Greeks and included artillery and siege apparatus. The artillery were called *'Tormenta'* with *'Ballistas'* like the large mounted crossbows which fired arrows loaded into grooves, *'Scorpions'* that fired bolts up to 500 yards, *'Carrobillistas'*, which were pulled on wheels by two horses and *'Catapults'* capable of hurling large stones. There were also many types of siege engines including metal-plated timber-framed assault towers over 35 metres tall, battering rams often mounted inside towers with iron 'ram head' terminals, and many other tools for demolition.

So how did the individual Roman soldier's appearance alter through the centuries?

1) 700 BC: Very early Roman infantry may well have worn a very simple helmet, carried a round Greek style shield, a single-edged or one piece bronze sword, a thrusting spear and a plain tunic or nothing at all. No armour was worn except by officers.

2) 500 BC: Soldiers now look very much more like the Greek *'hoplites'* wearing Corinthian type helmets, muscle armour and leg armour of bronze, a round shield of bronze or hide about 2 feet wide, and a single-edged sword called a *'kopis'*. Spears were about 12 feet long and first class Legionaries would have fought in a Greek *'phalanx'* formation.

3) 200 BC: The Legionary becomes a front line soldier equipped with a short thrusting *'Gladius'* sword (possibly copied from the Celts), throwing *'Pilum'* spear and a dagger. His armour still only comprises a bronze chest plate and an Etrusco-Corinthian helmet augmented with an oval-convex shield of wood and hide.

4) 55 BC: The 4,500 men of the Ninth Legion that accompanied Julius Caesar would have resembled the soldiers of period 3) when the unit was formed. The weapons were very similar to 3) but *'Lorica Hamate'* chain mail armour had been introduced.

5) 120 AD: This is the time of Hadrian, just after the Ninth Legion disappeared from York. *'Pilum'* spears have become weighted with a lead ball just below the metal shaft of the javelin possibly to stop horses and chariots, the dagger has been discarded but the sword is the same as 4). The armour is now the classic *'Lorica Segmentata'* made from metal strips, the helmet is the *'Cross Bun'* type noted for its neck protection, and the shield has become the well-known curved rectangle. A 'Legion' now comprises about 6,000 men.

6) 200 AD: Legionaries of this period wear much heavier helmets with greater face protection and armour with fewer but larger plates which is more comfortable to wear. The *'Pilum'* is gradually being superseded by a thrusting spear and the *'Gladius'* sword has been replaced by the much longer *'Spatha'* which gives greater reach in horse-mounted combat and when trying to strike an opponent on a horse.

7) 300 AD: In the third century AD the Roman Empire passed through many upheavals ultimately leading to a reduction in the size of the Legions and the end of standardized military equipment. Frequently the distinctive *'Lorica Segmentata'* armour was replaced by chain mail, the *'Cross Bun'* helmet by one derived from Persian origins, and the shield by a round one – both more familiar features of the Early Medieval 'Dark Ages'. The long sword and thrusting spear, however, remained much the same.

8) 400 AD: By now a 'Legion' is reduced to about 1,000 men and the Legionaries are equipped to deal mainly with horse-

mounted Barbarians. The spear is longer with a much broader point and the helmet has a raised protective ridge on top. The long sword is worn on the left side and the shield is much larger with throwing darts strapped inside, a feature more familiar to Saxon period warfare. Armour is no longer used except by heavy infantry units.

With the successive refinements of the Roman tools of war it could be expected that the Roman war machine would almost always be victorious – but history shows that this was not so. In fact some amazingly talented and determined foes stood defiant in the face of both Caesar and Empire.

VI

THE ROMAN REPUBLIC ENCOUNTERS THE HELVETI

By 75 BC the Roman Republic began to expand into Europe and encountered particular difficulties with the tribes of southern Gaul (now France), especially the Allobrogues of *'Provinca Narbonensis'* which is now known as modern day Provence.

It is thought that the Ninth Legion or *'Legio IX Hispanic'* was one of the units formed to deal with the Gaulish problem and that they took part in all Julius Caesar's Gallic campaigns, being frequently singled out for distinguished service and adding many trophies to their standards. They eventually became known as *'Singulans Virtutis Verterrima'* or one of the best fighting Legions in the whole of Caesar's army.

Caesar began his campaigns in 58 BC as the result of alarming reports reaching Rome of a massive migration by the Helveti tribe from what is now modern day Switzerland into the southern parts of Gaul. This affected two provinces subject to Rome, *'Cisalpine Gaul'*, now northern Italy, and *'Transalpine Gaul'* covering Southern Provence. As Caesar was the Governor of Cisalpine Gaul and the unbounded region of Transalpine Gaul, he took full advantage of the situation to further his political ambitions and, at the inexperienced military age of 41, went to war.

Initially the advance of the Helveti had taken him completely by surprise, but he ordered the Legion stationed in Gaul and a large force of Auxiliaries raised in Northern Italy to march north to face them. The move paid off and the Helveti halted at the River Rhone where Caesar's forces had constructed fortifications and removed the only bridge. It rapidly became apparent to

Caesar that the Helveti had in excess of 100,000 warriors and he was vastly out-numbered. In response he returned to Italy where he had already raised three new Legions and to this he added two more, eventually creating the 'Twelfth XII', 'Seventh VII', 'Eleventh XI', 'Eighth VIII' and 'Tenth X' to join the existing 'Ninth IX' from Gaul.

Taking his new Legions plus Auxiliaries, he marched back to the fortifications on the Rhone to find that the Helveti had enlisted the aid of a local Aedvan Chieftain called Dumnorix who had negotiated safe passage for them over the River Saone and across the lands of the 'Sequani'. Caesar then took the Tenth, Seventh, and Ninth, and marched through the night to the new river crossing at the Saone where he attacked, wiping out most of those Helveti who had crossed, capturing all their baggage and scattering the survivors into the surrounding forests. The Legionary engineers then constructed a stone bridge over the Saone in a day.

Weakened by the loss of warriors and supplies, the Helveti sued for peace and Caesar responded with reasonable terms but, unknown to him, the Helveti had forged a political alliance with the local 'Aedus' tribe. Being wisely suspicious, Caesar decided to shadow the Helveti with scouts while leaving his main force several miles behind to deter the Helveti from

plundering the countryside; then supplies he had been promised by the Aeduans failed to materialize. In addition the site of the Helvetian camp was very large and unsuitable for battle and a false report that the Helvetian army was encamped by a hill only 7 miles away left Caesar with no choice but to go in search of supplies.

He consulted his second-in-command Labienus, communicated his displeasure with the Aedui, and set off for their capital at Bibracte with a view to obtaining the supplies which they were withholding. Seeing the direction the Roman army was departing, the Helveti began to harass the Roman rear-guard, but Caesar was simply biding his time. As soon as he reached a suitable battle ground with a small hill he halted his forces and

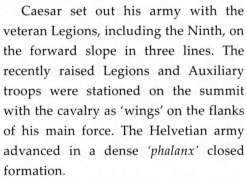

turned to give battle.

Caesar set out his army with the veteran Legions, including the Ninth, on the forward slope in three lines. The recently raised Legions and Auxiliary troops were stationed on the summit with the cavalry as 'wings' on the flanks of his main force. The Helvetian army advanced in a dense *'phalanx'* closed formation.

The Roman Cavalry charged but were easily brushed aside by the tightly packed-warriors, who crashed into the veteran legions on the lower slopes. Once close combat was engaged the Legionaries let fly their javelins and the Helvetian front lines fell. Urged on by their Centurions, they then ploughed in with their thrusting swords driving the Helvetians back almost a mile. Suddenly the Helvetian rearguard appeared on the Roman flank, cutting off the Ninth and Tenth Legions and creating a battle on two fronts which raged on into the night. Despite their best efforts the Helvetis could not break the disciplined Roman lines and they gradually fell, surrendered or fled to neighbouring tribes.

Caesar then proclaimed that anyone found harbouring Helveti refugees would be attacked and marched back to the Rhine where 5,000 escaping Helveti were stopped and executed. Any remaining Helveti were then allowed to return home to Switzerland.

The loss of life had been appallingly high with records of the time claiming that out of the 370,000 men, women and children who had started out westward, only 115,000 returned. 255,000 were dead or missing. The remains of the Ninth Legion returned to Northern Italy to rest and recruit more Legionaries.

VII

THE ROMAN REPUBLIC ENCOUNTERS THE GERMANS

Shortly after the defeat of the Helveti, Caesar faced another problem in Gaul. In earlier times the Sequani had hired 17,000 German warriors to aid them in their inter-tribal wars, a manoeuvre that had seriously backfired when they had to forfeit a third of their lands when the Germans decided to stay. The Germans, under king Ariovistus, then wanted to increase their land holdings by another third at which point the Sequani appealed to Caesar for help. Caesar responded by sending an envoy who was sent packing by Ariovistus with a message telling Caesar in no uncertain terms to stay out of German affairs or the Romans would be the worse off for it.

This was a clear and direct threat to the Romans which came at a time when reports were coming in of more Germans crossing the Rhine into Roman territory. Once again the Legions were told to march with newly-trained men in the ranks bringing them back to full strength. German forces were heading for the Sequani town of Vesontio, which was well supplied and could not be allowed to fall into their hands.

Caesar marched night and day and occupied the town but, unfortunately, the reputation of the German warriors had preceded them and the local Gauls began to spread frightening tales throughout the Roman camp.

Caesar was told that the Legions would refuse to march under their young officers so he called all the Centurions to a Council of War where he told them he would personally take the Tenth Legion and face the barbarians – alone if necessary! The Centurions of the Ninth Legion declared they would also join him and, by early morning, Caesar left with all his army in tact.

When King Ariovistus was notified of the Roman advance he sent envoys to Caesar and a meeting was arranged, proved entirely fruitless, and was called off when the King's German bodyguard attacked Caesar's mounted officers. Ariovistus then marched his forces round the Roman encampment cutting off Caesar's supply lines, but refused to engage the Romans in battle despite repeated attempts to draw him into conflict. Interrogated German prisoners provided the answer – Ariovistus believed he would lose a pitched battle if he engaged the Romans before the new moon appeared! This was a stroke of good luck for Caesar.

He rested his six Legions until the Germans had established their camp, then forced a march to the location taking the Germans completely by surprise. Placing their women and children behind their army in wagons, the Germans engaged the Romans on their left wing, Caesar's right, the location of the Ninth and Tenth Legions.

German lines broke but the Romans' other wing, Caesar's left, was in trouble and was being pushed back. Caesar failed to notice the developing problem as he was far too busy with the fighting on the right wing. Seeing the danger, accounts describe how a young unnamed cavalry officer called up the Roman reserves and effectively saved the battle. The Germans fled back to the River Rhine with the Roman Cavalry in pursuit and very few made it across. Ariovistus found a boat and made the crossing but many women and children were captured and sold by Caesar as slaves back in Italy. Ariovistus was right to watch the moon for it held his defeat in its grasp!

The battle-hardened Ninth Legion wintered in southern Gaul and began the process of regrouping and training more Legionaries once again.

VIII

THE ROMAN REPUBLIC ENCOUNTERS THE BELGAE

During the winter, reports reached Caesar of a northern Gaulish tribe called the *'Belgae'* making preparations for a major military campaign, preparations which were in danger of spreading to other tribes in Roman-controlled Gaul. Caesar raised two more Legions in the spring of 57 BC and marched north for a couple of weeks, crossing the River Aisne in an attempt to face the Belgae forces, which were also now on the move.

The Belgae would not give battle, but instead concentrated on trying to cut off Roman supply routes. Roman Cavalry and archers cleared these small Belgae forces and crossed the river to remove others. Unknown to Caesar, the following night the Belgae began to retreat and, by morning, they were gone. The potential battlefield was deserted!

Caesar sent the Cavalry after them while following with three Legions picking off any Belgae forces he caught up with, until they were back in their original tribal territory. Here the Belgae obtained submissive terms from every tribe except the *'Nervis'*, a warrior people who refused to reach terms with either them or the Romans.

Accordingly the Romans marched north towards the River Sambre, crossed with Cavalry and Archers, and attacked the waiting Nervi Cavalry. Whilst this was taking place, Nervi Foot Soldiers hid in the woods and observed the arrival of the first Legions till late in the day. As evening drew near the Nervi flooded out of the woods in large numbers and attacked the Roman cavalry with such ferocity that they were driven off the battlefield, then turned and crossed the river, surprising the main Roman forces.

Despite this massed attack the Romans recovered and the Ninth and Tenth Legions on the left flank drove the Nervi back into the river where a great number perished below the waves.

The Eighth and Eleventh Legions met with similar success, but the Twelfth and Seventh on the right flank had become detached and surrounded. At this point the two rearguard Legions arrived with the baggage train and joined in the attack. The Tenth also rallied to the aid of the Twelfth and Seventh, followed by the Ninth, who had finished dispatching the Nervi in the river. The Ninth distinguished itself by excelling in javelin throwing and, of about 60,000 Nervi, only 1,000 survived to crawl from the battlefield.

IX

HOME TO FACE THE VENETI

After the victory over the Nervi, the Ninth Legion marched back to Italy with Caesar, while the Twelfth Legion headed to the area around Lake Geneva under Commander Servius Galba to conduct a campaign in the Alps. This was unsuccessful and the Twelfth were eventually withdrawn as the pacification of the Gaulish peoples was felt to have reached a satisfactory level.

The Ninth Legion remained at their winter camp in northern Italy and the men hoped for more relaxed times. Their wish was not to be.

In 56 BC war broke out again along the Atlantic Coast in a region known as the Andes. The Seventh Legion were using this region as a Winter camp and had sent envoys out to local tribes in order to obtain the necessary food and supplies but the 'Veneti' had, instead, detained them as prisoners. Caesar was informed and he replied with instructions to build warships on the River Loire without delay.

Captains and crews were enlisted and the Ninth Legion ordered to march north to join the gathering Roman forces. It is thought that Caesar utilized the services of friendly Gallic sailors and placed his best Javelineers and Archers on the ships. If this hypothesis is correct then the Ninth Legion would have seen service on Caesar's ships. Much to Caesar's consternation it was soon discovered that the enemy strongholds along the Loire were impossible to assault directly by river, as the strong tides turned every 12 hours thwarting navigation.

Not to be deterred, the Romans built huge dikes in an attempt to keep the sea back, but the Veneti simply brought up a fleet of their own ships to take defenders to their strongest defensive positions, tactics which they continued throughout the summer months.

In response the Roman ships attacked with grappling irons. The ships of the Veneti depended on sail and did not use oars so the grappling irons tore off their sails and rigging leaving them as sitting ducks for the Roman Archers and Javelineers.

The Veneti eventually lost over 200 ships and enough men to cause their surrender upon which Caesar had their counsellors executed and the entire tribe sold into slavery.

Significantly for future campaigns, the Ninth Legion had now spent some time working on ships creating a perfect seaborne invasion force to support Caesar's later plans.

X

CAESAR MEETS CASSIVELLAUNUS

In 55 BC Caesar called on the engineers of the Ninth Legion to help construct a military bridge over the River Rhine. He then marched over it, burnt villages, destroyed crops, subjugated the remaining German tribes, and returned across the bridge destroying it as he went. It was the end of a long European Summer and Caesar's conquering eye turned to Britain. During his Gallic campaigns the Gauls had received reinforcements from the British tribes on the south coast and this had been duly noted.

Weeks before the planned invasion rumours about a prosperous Britain were circulating through the Legions. The land promised wealth.

In the Ninth Legion one of the Centurions told his men that *"all the women in Britain were fair haired – the redheads who caused trouble amongst the slave dealers in Rome and fetched a bad price in the slave markets were non existent."*

Another, a Greek, told his men that Britain was *"... the last outpost of Atlantis, the magnificent civilization which had sunk beneath the waves 7000 years before, but Atlantean colonists still inhabited its shores and lived in wealthy cities."*

Julius Caesar's army, which had subjugated some of the best armies in Europe and Asia, gathered at Witsand near Calais, and on the 5th August 55 BC crossed the narrow waters of the Channel in two divisions.

Evidently Caesar planned a short raid as he only took two Legions with him, the Seventh and the Tenth; the Ninth remained in Gaul with the others in reserve, protecting the Roman ports along the northern coast. The campaign was a short disaster!

The Roman fleet failed to find a secure harbour and a bad storm in the English Channel destroyed many ships. Caesar's cavalry did not arrive at all. Fifty-five days later, having penetrated only seven miles inland and having experienced a military defeat of major proportions, Caesar returned with his army to the comparative safety of the continent. It was the closing months of 55 BC.

10th May 54 BC, the following year, Caesar returned to Britain with a larger force of five Legions including the Ninth, 2,000 cavalry and a fleet of over 800 vessels.

It is thought they landed, unopposed, somewhere between Deal and Ramsgate as the Britons had withdrawn inland to observe the invasion forces and draw up a defensive position behind the River Stour. The Romans had to cross this river under heavy attack, but were able to drive the Britons out of their defensive positions and up to Bigbury where the Britons regrouped. The Seventh Legion breached the outer defences of Bigbury but the Britons withdrew and regrouped again.

The Ninth Legion were about to advance on their flank when news came that, once again, a storm in the Channel had damaged the fleet sinking 43 ships and all forces were to return immediately to the coast and begin repairs. This gave the Britons time to reorganize and form a new army under the leadership of a chief called Cassivellaunus.

When Caesar resumed his offensive by moving inland, the Britons attacked in force as his Legions halted to make camp. The Ninth Legion suffered losses in equipment and manpower as the Britons attacked in wave after wave of organized cavalry and light-weight chariots. The Legions locked shields and held a defensive line until the Roman cavalry were able to break out and rout the British.

In response Cassivellaunus withdrew his forces beyond the River Thames and set about constructing a stockade and underwater barrier of sharpened stakes at the ford near Kingston. The Roman cavalry had little problem forcing a passage through these hastily erected defences and the relentless Roman war machine ploughed on northwards and into the lands of the *'Trinovantes'*.

As it turned out the Trinovantes assisted the Roman forces, who then advanced on Verulamium (St Albans), the timber-walled and ditched stronghold of Cassivellaunus himself. Attacking on two sides, Caesar's forces easily captured the stronghold with much booty, and Cassivellaunus had little choice but to sue for peace. Caesar gave him easy terms, imposed a tribute, carried off captives and hostages, but failed to make any provision for the occupation of his captured territory by Roman troops.

On 10th September 54 BC Caesar finally concluded a hasty and ignominious peace at St Albans. In this second invasion it is thought that over a thousand ships were used and five Legions; some put the number of troops at 60,000 men.

In his *'A Description of the British People'* found in Caesar's *'Gallic War – Volume 2'* he wrote: *"Most of the inland inhabitants do not sow corn, but live on milk and flesh, and are clad in skins. All the Britons, indeed, dye themselves with wood which occasions a bluish colour, and thereby have a more terrible appearance in fight."*

The Legions then returned to their remaining vessels, which scarcely held them, and sailed back to Gaul.

It has been said that the 54 BC 'invasion' was a military 'probe' or advance party, but the numbers of ships and troops were too great for that to be the case and the Roman writer Dion Cassius tells us that Caesar had intended to carry the war into the interior of Britain but found his force inadequate to meet the British opposition. As a direct result of the Britons pulling Roman spears out of themselves and throwing them back, the Romans modified the 'pilum' spear to incorporate a bending point!

Julius Caesar and his army were so thoroughly beaten by the British forces that the Romans were to threaten and posture for almost a hundred years before finding the courage to return. Despite being supported by two divisions of Rome's best fighting troops Caesar was only able to penetrate around seventy miles inland against a British resistance which he subsequently described as *"painted savages"*!

The real reasons for Caesar's retreat are lost in the mists of time. Was the island realm of Britain not thought wealthy enough for them to occupy, or was the military response from the Celtic Britons far greater than Caesar had anticipated? And what of Britain's navy in this period, did they play some part in the destruction of Caesar's ships out in the channel? One thing is for certain, Roman accounts of Caesar's campaigns are certainly bias in favour of the conquering Romans, but still show ample evidence that the peoples of this island were not to be trifled with.

XI

CAESAR MEETS VERCINGETORIX

Continental Gaul was almost subdued when, in 52 BC, a Gallic prince named Vercingetorix united many tribes against the might of Rome and cut the supply and communication lines to Caesar's forces including the Ninth Legion.

Caesar, who was wintering in Cisalpine Gaul at this time, duly responded and marched north, defeating some of the warring tribes and joining the Legions who had been cut off.

Vercingetorix then made the grave error of confronting the Roman forces instead of using the guerrilla tactics preferred by previous Gallic leaders. Now reunited, Roman forces including the Ninth Legion soundly defeated the Gauls, driving Vercingetorix back to the stronghold town of Alesia. Here the Gauls felt confident of holding the town on a hill with steep and treacherous slopes and they knew that reinforcements were on the way – but the battle for Alesia was to change the face of Europe for ever.

At Alesia Caesar set up twenty-five temporary holding camps around the hills between the River Oserain and the River Ose. His forces were over 70,000 strong and consisted of his best veteran Legions, the Seventh, Eighth, Ninth and Tenth, under his personal command.

The Romans then set about a massive engineering feat never before undertaken on such a scale. They dug two twenty-foot deep ditches around the complete defences of Alesia turning the town from a stronghold to a prison. One ditch they filled with water and the other with wooden spikes and an added earthbank topped with a timber wall and towers. These barriers ran round Alesia for a colossal 12 miles containing Vercingetorix

and his forces.

Then Caesar turned his attention to the impending Gaulish reinforcements, building 15 miles of outer defences placing his Roman Legions between these and the two rings of ditches. As Caesar surveyed his vast military undertaking he must have felt that victory was already assured and Celtic Europe was finally his, but the taking of an entire continent is never a forgone conclusion.

8,000 cavalry and almost 250,000 infantry arrived as reinforcements on the side of Vercingetorix – and that's by Caesar's own estimate! Although this figure may be an overestimation it certainly conveys Caesar's feelings on the matter. Vercingetorix must have smiled a wry Celtic smile through his drooping Gallic moustache and beard as this time it was he who surveyed the sea of Gauls swaying beyond the now feeble-looking Roman defensive lines.

Without further delay he sent his troops out of Alesia to attack the Romans and fill in the ditches, but Caesar acted quickly and sent Roman cavalry to drive back the Gallic horsemen.

The next day the Gaulish army of reinforcements sent 60,000 infantry behind a nearby hill to rest until midday. As the main army attacked the Romans from the front the infantry emerged and attacked from behind. Added to this, Vercingetorix realized what was happening and sent his own troops to attack along the defensive lines. His next move would be to try to break out of Alesia and join the attack on the Roman forces. The situation was critical for the Romans.

The Ninth Legion formed up in two lines, one facing inwards and one outwards, and were being pressed by Gauls on all sides. Caesar sent his second-in-command, Labienus, and 3,000 men to help the hard-pressed Ninth and their line held.

His cavalry was then sent to attack the Gauls from the rear, who wrongly believed that this constituted another much larger Roman army arriving to help Caesar. Gallic forces panicked and fled sealing Vercingetorix's fate. Roman Legionaries and cavalry did what they did best and the day belonged to them.

Next day Vercingetorix personally surrendered to Caesar and was led away in chains. Such threats to Roman superiority were shown no pity. Although his fate is unknown, it is thought that this magnificent and determined Celtic warrior-chief may have been ritually strangled as part of Caesar's victory parade through Rome in accordance with the custom of such events.

The rest of the captured Gauls were given to the Legions as

slaves, along with captured booty. It is said that every man in the Ninth Legion had his own personal Gaul for a slave, but many sold them to the slave traders of Rome.

A year after the battle the Gauls made one final attempt to drive the Romans out but failed again. About sixty Celtic Chieftains were assembled before Caesar and agreed to terms which made Gaul a Roman province in 51 BC.

Rome grew from a Mediterranean Empire to a European Empire and, in so doing, brought about the beginning of the end for the Celtic speaking world. The Ninth Legion's silver eagle standard was retired after the battle of Alesia and a new one supplied made from solid gold.

XII

Trouble in the Camp

By far the worst enemy of Romans were the Romans themselves, and in Rome there were growing fears about Caesar. The ambitions of this man were endless. He now expected to be given executive power over Rome and her growing Empire but the Senate refused, so hardly surprisingly Caesar marched on Rome. The city descended into panic and Caesar's main opponent, General Pompey, withdrew his forces from Italy to gain more time to train them and recruit. It was the eve of civil war.

At this time the Ninth Legion were stationed at the town of Placentia on the River Po in Cisalpine Gaul. Word reached them of the developing situation in Rome and they violently mutinied against Caesar.

On hearing this, Caesar was so angry that he ordered the Legion disbanded. Only the council of Mark Anthony saved it. The ring leaders were rounded up and punished instead, and the Legion survived to be moved to Spain.

Here they met and fought the troops of General Pompey, Roman against Roman. Having charged the town they were badly mauled and cut off from the rest of the forces loyal to Caesar. Fighting for five hours, losing seventy men, and sustaining over a hundred casualties, they were finally relieved. The victory eventually went to Caesar's forces and the Ninth marched on to northern Greece under the command of Lentulus Marcellinius. While at Dyrrachium, Lentulus is thought to have become ill and Caesar sent Flavius Postumus to assist him, but Lentulus' problems had only just begun.

The Ninth Legion had made camp by the sea when suddenly,

at dawn, the troops under General Pompey attacked overpowering some of the Cohorts. The Standard Bearer was seriously wounded and gave the Ninth Legion's new golden eagle to a cavalry officer to be taken to Caesar for safety. Lentulus Marcellinus sent reinforcements to help the Ninth but these too were pushed back.

Word was sent to Mark Anthony who was at a nearby outpost and he marched with twelve Cohorts of men and checked the enemy forces. Nevertheless Caesar had lost 960 soldiers, 32 military Tribunes and Centurions, and 4 Roman knights, primarily from the Ninth Legion. Pompey's General Labienus, who had deserted Caesar at the start of the civil war, killed all prisoners from the Ninth Legion in front of the Pompeian army and, when this was later reported to the men of the Ninth, they took an oath of vengeance against Labienus.

General Pompey finally met Caesar at Pharsalus in Northern Greece. The Ninth Legion was on the left wing under the command of Mark Anthony but so depleted that the Eight Legion joined them to make one, with both Legions ordered to co-operate with each other. In the ensuing battle Caesar's army soundly defeated the Pompeian army. Pompey fled to Egypt, to the court of King Ptolemy (a boy king), who invited him aboard his boat and then had him killed. Caesar followed, landed in Egypt, and was famously given Pompey's head in a vase!

Reinforced with fresh troops, the Ninth Legion moved to Africa and fought alongside the Tenth Legion in this campaign. At the battle of Thapsus they again fought on the left flank with the Eight Legion, and again they were victorious. Caesar was winning the war.

Caesar now moved to Spain for the final act of the civil war. In 45 BC, on the 17th of March, the great Battle of Munda was fought in an area of Northern Spain. The Ninth Legion were involved and, after the defeat of the enemy in which 30,000 men were killed, the hated general Labienus fell off his horse whilst fleeing the battle to be slain by the cavalry of the Ninth Legion. They then stormed the town of Corduba killing over 20,000 of the occupants. The oath of vengeance against Labienus had been carried out and the Ninth Legion is thought to have publicly burnt his body on the battlefield at Munda. The civil war was over.

Caesar returned to Rome and the Senate offered to make him King, but Caesar replied: *"I am not King but Caesar."* He was declared 'dictator in perpetuity' and great celebrations followed in his honour.

Caesar seems to have paid little heed to flattery, and went on with his plans for consolidating the great Roman dominions.

In 53 BC the Parthians (who came from modern day Iran) had destroyed most of a Roman army under the command of the proconsul of Syria, Marcus Licinius Crassus. The Parthians had always been, and remained, a threat to the Roman Empire in the East. Caesar's plan was simple: leave Mark Anthony in charge of Italy and invade the Parthian lands emulating Alexander the Great's magnificent campaign, and then drive on into India. The Ninth Legion was to be part of this great expedition to the East and was moved into position with other veterans in readiness.

But, Caesar had many enemies, and the civil war had cost thousands of Roman lives. He had also brought his foreign mistress to Rome, the Egyptian Queen Cleopatra, who had helped in his campaigns. This proved to be a very unpopular move.

A conspiracy led by Brutus and Cassius assassinated Julius Caesar on the 15th of March 44 BC. The Ninth Legion was then left to his heir Octavian, who later became the Emperor Augustus.

XIII

THE KNOWN HISTORY OF THE NINTH LEGION UNDER THE EMPEROR

Octavian, a youth of eighteen years and Caesar's principal heir, was at Apollonia in Ilyria pursuing his studies and preparing to join the approaching campaign against the Parthians. His friend Vipsanius Agrippa advised him to place himself at the head of the Legions which had been gathered together for the forthcoming campaign, but Octavian was determined to go at once to Rome and take his inheritance, entirely contrary to the advice of all his nearest relatives. The Ninth Legion, who now came under the command of Octavian, remained in situ as their new commander rushed to Rome.

Upon Octavian's arrival in Rome he presented himself before Mark Anthony and declared that he would accept Caesar's 'Will' and the 'Clause of Adoption', and desired the private fortunes of the dictator Caesar be handed over to him.

Anthony was embarrassed since he had already dealt with Caesar's estate and, after the two months it had taken Octavian to come to Rome, very little of it was left. Worse than this Anthony was unable to give account of it and claimed it was owed to him anyway!

Roman politics being what they were, Anthony might have been able to put this young man out of his way if his own conduct had not roused enemies against him. Octavian decided to join Anthony, and was allowed to do so as the Republicans under Brutus and Cassius were convinced that, after the overthrow of Mark Anthony (which was their first objective), they would be able to put the young Octavian aside.

The history of the Ninth Legion here is uncertain, but another civil war was about to begin and over 40 Legions were eventually involved.

It is thought that the Ninth joined Octavian in Lower Italy, but then Octavian joined Mark Anthony in Macedonia and the Ninth went with him to deliver a decisive blow against Brutus and Cassius. First of all Cassius was beaten by Mark Anthony – but at almost the same time Brutus defeated the army of Octavian. The Ninth Legion were inevitably involved in the action and suffered losses with Octavian's military camp eventually being captured. Cassius, under the mistaken impression that Brutus had also been defeated, killed himself.

Brutus met the army of Anthony, now joined by Octavian and his forces, at the Battle of Philippi in 42 BC. The Ninth Legion was now under the command of Mark Anthony himself and Brutus was defeated, dying by his own hand after the battle.

Valerius Messulla, Brutus' second-in-command, surrendered the remnants of the Republican's army and all of Caesar's murderers who could be captured were executed. The other Republican officers received pardons while ordinary soldiers were drafted into the ranks of the victorious Legions, the Ninth receiving some of these soldiers into its depleted ranks. In addition to this many of the veterans were now entitled to a discharge, 170,000 in all, and some of the veterans from the Ninth Legion did choose this point to retire, most to lands promised to them in Italy.

The Roman Empire was growing at a fast pace. Cisalpine Gaul was joined to Italy, Octavian received the Spanish Provinces, and Mark Anthony, the real victor at Philippi, received the lands of Narbonensis.

Anthony went on to Asia. Everywhere he set up or deposed client kings and made arrangements generally according to his own pleasure. He summoned the Queen of Egypt, Cleopatra, before him at Tarsus. Cleopatra had received precise information on the character of Anthony, and appeared before him in

Tarsus as the goddess Aphrodite, immediately succeeding in captivating him. However, back in Italy, Octavian had problems.

Veterans who had retired, some from the Ninth, moved into lands confiscated from large landowners who were left to bear the cost. In the year 41 BC one of the consuls and brother of Mark Anthony, Lucius Antonius, disapproved of the whole measure. Octavian supported the veterans and resolved to carry out the soldier's wishes, but Lucius Antonius was not acting independently of support and these matters resulted in another actual war. Antonius was besieged in Persia by Octavian and Agrippa – but Mark Anthony in Egypt did nothing.

The Ninth Legion was probably involved on the side of Octavian. Persia, after a desperate resistance of five months, was forced to capitulate. Antonius, out of consideration for his brother, received safe conduct away from the conflicts in defeat. Anthony received the news that Persia had been captured and that Octavian was growing hostile towards his lieutenants owing to their ambivalent and unsupportive behaviour.

Anthony returned to Italy and they met towards the end of the summer of 40 BC. It was decided that reconciliation between the two great men was to be cemented by the marriage of Mark Anthony with Octavia, half sister to Octavian, Anthony's previous wife having died in Greece. Anthony now went to Syria to stop the Parthians who, in the 30's BC, made attacks on Syria and Hither Asia.

The Parthians were beaten back and retired to their own country after they had lost in various battles and losing Pacorus, the son of their king, in 38 BC. Again, the whereabouts of the Ninth Legion at this time is uncertain, but must be assumed to be still under the command of Octavian.

Anthony now planned to continue the campaign Julius Caesar was about to take into the Parthian homelands just before his assassination. Whilst preparations for the Parthian war were proceeding, Octavian was establishing himself in the West and nearly all the forces in this part of the Roman Empire had gone over to his side and to which he had added a large fleet.

Anthony's campaign against the Parthians failed in 36 BC ending in a calamitous retreat due to the fact he had started out too late in the year and his Armenian allies had let him down. He had received very few reinforcements from the West and did not disguise his annoyance at this. But he still had his secret weapon, Queen Cleopatra of Egypt, as his friend and ally. When he summoned her to meet him at Antioch he once again became infatuated with her, an infatuation which proved stronger than the political reasons that rendered his marriage to Octavia so important. Octavia tried to win back her husband but Anthony went to Alexandria with Cleopatra and ruled from there as her husband instead, leading to a war of honour between Octavian and Anthony.

Both men had established huge areas of Empire; Anthony in 35 BC was occupied in Armenia where he hoped to avenge upon the king the disasters of the Parthian war. Later in 34 BC he was to bring him as his prisoner to Alexandria. He then turned all his attention to the West, where the final struggle for Roman supremacy could no longer be postponed.

Octavian in Italy had done much to increase his popularity. At Rome a new water supply was provided and his able friend, Agrippa, kept the army and fleet in good order. The Ninth Legion were involved in campaigns in Dalatria and Istria in order to give a more advantageous frontier to Upper Italy. In 32 BC Octavian officially declared war on Egypt at a time when the

Ninth Legion remained under his command. Meanwhile, Anthony meditated on a landing in Italy in order to bring the war to an end there, and then upon how to seize the city of Rome itself.

Mark Anthony, who in the campaigns against the Parthians had shown himself once more to be a brave soldier and successful General, thought that the issue should be decided by a land battle. However, Queen Cleopatra, who was strongest in her ships – commanding 300 war galleys, insisted on a sea fight. In any case if Anthony wanted to cross over to Italy, a victory at sea was a necessity if he was to succeed. Many of his commanders wanted a land battle as they felt that there was a deficiency of competent sailors. Many inexperienced soldiers would have to go on board ships and his commanders slowly started to desert.

With Octavian everything was still going well. He had very capable leaders and Agrippa, who'd shown his worth on land and sea, was chosen to command Octavian's fleet whilst he made preparations to march through Syria for an impending land war.

In the spring of 31 BC Agrippa took the offensive and was successful in some naval operations, whilst the land forces faced each other in a temporary stand-off without fighting. The Ninth Legion was in Syria under Octavian at this time.

On 2nd September 31 BC a great sea battle was fought off the promontory of Actium. Mark Anthony was defeated and Cleopatra made for the open sea during the fight. Anthony, in his infatuation, hastened after her. This was the end for Mark Anthony.

A few days later the land army, left without a leader, surrendered. The soldiers of Anthony now acknowledged Octavian as their commander. Anthony reached Egypt. He now only had the Twelfth Legion and a few other remnants left, all of whom soon deserted. As Octavian reached Egypt in 30 BC, his other commander, Gallus, attacked from Cyrene. In July Anthony took his own life and the Ninth Legion reached Alexandria with Octavian on the 1st of August.

Cleopatra had an interview with Octavian but found in him no mercy – she was, after all, the intentional usurper of his half-sister! Soon after this she was confined to quarters and took her own life, legend has it, by suckling an asp (poisonous snake) to her bosom, perhaps a fitting end to a woman who had just cut short the world's oldest ruling dynasty. Egypt ceased to be a kingdom. Octavian allowed himself to be hailed as 'Pharaoh'. Egypt just another Roman province.

Octavian was now the sole ruler of the whole Roman Empire. In the year 27 BC the Senate conferred on him the additional name of *'Augustus'* meaning 'Exalted' and he was in the future officially called *'Imperator Caesar Augustus'*. From now on all those who followed Augustus were called 'Caesar'.

XIV

THE RULE OF THE CAESARS

After the Battle of Actium and the end of the civil war with Mark Anthony, Augustus reduced the number of Legions back down to about 30 and, at this time, the Ninth Legion formed part of this regular army.

In 26 BC Augustus Caesar took personal command of the war in Spain against the Cantabri. With him went two Legions to strengthen the Roman forces already there, the Fifth Legion – Legion V '*Alaudae*', and the Ninth Legion. It was in this campaign that the Ninth Legion served with great distinction and Augustus conferred on them the title of '*Hispana*'. (Not to be confused with the Ninth Legion being an entirely 'Spanish Legion' as there is no evidence for this.) In 25 BC Augustus became very ill and retired from personal command of the Legions, and Antistius Vetus, an able man, took over.

Now the Astures tribe attacked the Ninth Legion in the Astura River valley, but were forced back with heavy losses. The town of Lancia fell and the whole area was re-founded as a Roman colony for veterans. In 24 BC Augustus returned to Rome and the army in Spain was left to the command of Lucius Aemilius. Later on during that year the Cantabri and Astures tribes rebelled again and once again were defeated.

Hostilities were renewed in 22 BC and the Ninth and Fifth Legions took many prisoners. Other Roman forces were also involved under the command of Carisius and Furnius.

The Cantabrian prisoners were sold and legionaries made money on these, many of whom were sold to veterans. In 19 BC the Cantabrian prisoners of war rebelled, killed their masters and owners, returned to their lands and a revolt began again.

Augustus responded by sending Agrippa, the victor of Actium, who was by far his best general. Agrippa destroyed the Spanish uprising with utmost severity. By 18 BC the Fifth Legion V *'Alaudae'* was transferred to Germany and the Ninth Legion IX *'Hispana'* to Illyria and Spain was a stable Roman colony once again.

The Ninth Legion now came under the command of Tiberius and his brother Drusus and, between 16 and 12 BC, took part in the war in Pannonia and Dalmatia, a difficult mountainous region. In 9 BC they were pulled back to Ptus along with two other Legions, the Legio VIII *'Augusta'* and Legio XV *'Apollinaris'*. In 9 AD a great disaster befell the Roman army. Although the Ninth Legion were not involved, it had great significance for all the Legions.

In that year an insurrection broke out on the German frontier, largely owing to various failures by the incompetent governor Quinctilius Varus. The leader of the insurrection was a German Prince called Arminius who had been trained in Rome and had become a Roman Knight.

Quinctilius Varus decided to act and, in a move of extreme force, took the whole of his available army, Legions Seventeen, Eighteen and Nineteen plus many auxiliaries (over 30,000 men in total), in fact the whole of the main Roman army in Germany, into the Teutoburg Forest in pursuit of Arminius and his German tribes. Once in the Teutoberg Forest the unfavourable nature of the soil rendered treacherous by heavy rains and the blunders of Varus and his officers, brought about a

complete annihilation of all three Roman Legions and their auxiliaries. Only parts of the cavalry escaped.

As a result these three Legions disappeared forever out of the Imperial Army. Quinctilius Varus killed himself whilst many of the unfortunate Roman prisoners were massacred or sacrificed to Celtic Gods. When news reached Rome there was panic. Augustus withdrew his frontier from the Elbe to the Rhine. Tiberius was sent to hold the bridge on the Rhine. Many other Legions sent units to plug the gap left by the loss of the Seventeenth, Eighteenth and Nineteenth. Some of the Ninth Legion were almost certainly sent in these manoeuvres.

Later Germanicus, the son of Tiberius' brother Drusus, led an army into Germany with some success. He came across the slaughtered remains of Varus' army and buried them. One important outcome of this was that it was found that Roman chain mail armour had not stopped the heavy German spears from penetrating it and this led to an overall reappraisal of the Legion's equipment. During the next few years all the main Legions were re-equipped with armour made out of iron plates called 'Lorica Segmentata', other new equipment was introduced and existing equipment upgraded.

On the 19th of August 14 AD Augustus died. He was regarded as one of the world's greatest leaders in early history. The eventual form which Augustus gave to the Roman Empire remained in force for over 300 years.

At this time the Ninth Legion was at the garrison of Illyricum. Tiberius had started a mission to Illyricum when messengers rode in to inform him that Augustus was dying at Nola. Tiberius was then able to be on the spot when Augustus died and succeeded him as Caesar.

From the garrison at Illyricum, the Ninth Legion was transferred to North Africa in 20 AD where a deserter called Tacfarinas encouraged the Musulami tribes to revolt. This insurrection started to spread. The Ninth Legion appeared to have had a very difficult campaign and they did not return to Illyricum until 24 AD, where they remained until they were eventually transferred to the Province of Pannonia.

In 37 AD Tiberius Caesar died and Gaius Caesar, known as Caligula (because as a small boy he always wore 'red boots') became Caesar. Caligula was greeted with acclamations as the son of Germanicus and was heartily recognized by the Senate as Caesar. The new ruler also had a favourable reception from the army as a whole, and not just from the Legions on the Rhine.

However, Caligula soon proved not to be a mere 'incapable', but a homicidal madman!

The decisive turn for the worse came after a severe illness, possible caused by lead poisoning, lead being used extensively by the Romans in plumbing and utensils. After his recovery this demented youth proclaimed himself 'a god' and regarded himself as the *"fixed star round which the client kings should move like planets"* receiving from him various marks of favour. Herod Agrippa was famously provided with a principality in Biblical Judea. Ptolemueus, King of Mauritania, was granted the extraordinary privilege of issuing gold coins of his own. The princes of Armenia, Thrace and Commage also experienced his benevolent kindness.

Soon after this military affairs were also thrown into confusion by Caligula. In order to win laurels as a general he formed up a large army, which may well have included the Ninth Legion or part of it, and marched to Gaul and the Rhine where other legions joined him. After Caligula had obtained a treaty with the Chatti, a warlike tribe, he proceeded to the north coast of Gaul apparently in order to invade Britain. This entire expedition resulted in nothing as Caligula ordered troops to collect seashells on the beach as a tribute to the sea god.

Understandably this caused him to quarrel decisively with the commanding officers and he also made many enemies in the lower ranks by his numerous dismissals. Those who were in the intimate circle of the Emperor's friends were already aware that his state of mind was not normal and that, in the interests of the Empire and the Imperial house, he must be deposed.

This happened on the occasion of a state performance in the theatre on 24th January 41 AD. Caligula was struck down behind the scenes by Cassius Chaerea who was on security duty, and his wife Caesonia and her child were also killed ending his immediate dynasty. The next in line to be Caesar was Claudius.

It is said that, at the time of Caligula's murder, Claudius was found hiding behind a curtain in the palace! He was brought out into the camp of the Praetorian Guard a very frightened man, and here proclaimed Caesar.

Claudius, the son of the elder Drusus, was born at Lugdunum in 10 BC where his father was governor of Gaul. Weak-minded in youth, he had grown up among servants and had been carefully kept out of public sight in order not to compromise the dynasty. He had later become a diligent student and acquired much learning of which he made a display at inopportune moments. His long speeches in the Senate were dreaded and ridiculed and he was a great authority on Etruscan history. It was said he could speak the Etruscan language, the language of the primitive founders of Rome. In later ages Claudius' book on the Carthaginian wars was considered a masterpiece.

During this period of Roman history the real power lay with the freemen of the palace. The most conspicuous for their ability were Callistus who had kept the machinery of government working, Pallus who directed the finance department, and Narcissus who decided the foreign and home policy at the most critical moments. It was this Narcissus who decided to persuade

Claudius to invade Britain. He would choose the best Legions and the Ninth Legion was one of them.

XV

THE KNOWN HISTORY OF THE NINTH LEGION IN BRITAIN

Such was the reputation of British military force, its renown throughout Europe, and such was the Romans' fear of the British as a unique and effective fighting force, that initially Roman Legions mutinied saying: *"We will march anywhere in the world, but not out of it!"*

A) CONQUEST:

The backbone of the Claudian army chosen for the British invasion was made up of four main Legions, Legio II (Second) *'Augusta'* from Strasbourg, Legio XIV (Fourteen) *'Gemina'* from Mainz, the XX (Twentieth) *'Valera Victrix'* from Neuss, and the IX (Ninth) *'Hispana'* from Pannonia. The first three were all Rhine frontier Legions and had been troublesome in the recent past and, although good Legions, it may have been thought a good idea to transfer them to some other more volatile region to keep them fully occupied. However, the Ninth was considered the best Legion in the whole army at this time, and had continuously proved itself in recent wars.

The Commander chosen to lead this invasion was Aulus Plautius Silanus, a military man of great experience and Governor of Pannonia. Under Plautius were Lucius Sulpicius Galba (later to become Emperor), Flavius Sabinus his brother, Vespasian (who also later became Emperor), and Ghaeus Hosidius Geta who had commanded a Roman army successfully in Mauretania. These were amongst the best commanders in the Roman army.

The Ninth Legion accompanied Plautius on his journey from Pannonia to the embarkation camp at Boulogne, a distance of almost 800 miles with part of this journey being made by ship. By the time the Ninth had arrived, the other legions and auxiliary units were already there making a grand total of about 40,000 troops including 7,000 cavalry. But this magnificent Roman army ran into trouble almost immediately. First one of the principal generals, Galba, became ill.

Then the troops refused to embark on the ships, and many tales about the mysterious island of Britain started to run through the camps. Plautius was unable to convince the troops that these stories were untrue so he sent an envoy to the Emperor to ask for guidance and advice and awaited the Imperial envoy. Claudius sent Narcissus, a Greek freeman, and the troops were outraged when this ex-slave addressed them!

It is not known what Narcissus said, but they did eventually agree to the crossing and to campaigning in Britain. The crossing was made in three divisions and they landed on the Kent coast, making this the largest ever invasion of Britain.

In response the British tribes had massed about 70,000 men, which included 5,000 chariots, but with the Romans delaying the invasion the tribal armies disbanded to gather in their harvests. The Ninth Legion landed near Richborough on the coast of Kent and formed a bridgehead. Other landings were made near present day Dover. To the great surprise of the Romans no Britons appeared and they were able to land all their heavy equipment without hindrance. Although a clear advantage, this led to more speculation on the part of the Legions. What were the Britons planning and where were they?

The Ninth Legion was ordered inland. The Legate-in-Command was a man called Caesius Nasica. Still no Britons appeared! Scouts were sent out and were involved in a few skirmishes but the main British force had fallen back beyond the River Medway led by a king called Togodamnus and his brother

Caratacus.

On hearing that the main British force had been found near present day Aylesford, Plautius took most of his main force, leaving part of his auxiliary force to guard the bridgehead, and marched to meet them. As the Roman army reached the Medway they saw on the other side of the river a tribal army of about 70,000 to 80,000 men and well over 3,000 chariots. Plautius drew up his army. On the left he placed Legio II, next to them Legio XX, in the centre Legio IX, and on the right Legio XIV. The auxiliaries were placed in front of the Legions and the cavalry behind. The outcome of this battle was to change the face of British history.

Plautius moved the Legio II Augusta downstream and out of sight to build barges. On the right he sent units of Batavian cavalry who were trained to swim and ford rivers. With them went units of auxiliaries. How deep the River Medway was at the time is not known but the Batavian cavalry must have removed the heavy mail horse armour and possibly some human armour in order to ride across and attack. The same may have applied to the auxiliary troops. This unexpected attack took the British entirely by surprise. King Togodamnus hurled all his chariots and a large part of his foot soldiers at the cavalry attack.

Meanwhile Legio II Augusta were ferrying troops across the Medway on barges to the other side and, once formed up, they

attacked and units of Legio XX followed. The Britons were now being attacked on both sides. The Ninth Legion then crossed and was trying to encircle the Britons from the top. By nightfall on this first day Plautius had most of his troops on the British side of the Medway engaging the enemy in conflict.

On the second day the Britons

attacked the bridgehead, which was by now a pontoon bridge. The bridgehead commander, Hosidius Geta, was nearly captured but units of the Twentieth Legion held the bridgehead. Meanwhile the Ninth Legion had breached the British defensive line and mortally wounded King Togodamnus. The Britons withdrew and the battle was effectively lost.

The British forces retreated to the River Thames and crossed the mud flats to the other side. Roman cavalry tried to follow but became trapped in the dangerously soft ground and some riders were lost. The Romans then built a pontoon bridge further down the Thames, which was a much smaller river than it is today, and, after further skirmishes, established a base north of the Thames. The imperial order from Emperor Claudius then arrived ordering Plautius to await his coming.

Claudius brought with him a strong detachment of the Praetorian Guard and reinforcements from the Rhine Legions. They also brought elephants! The Emperor had not forgotten his history and how the elephants of Carthaginian General Hannibal had caused the Roman army so much trouble 250 years before. The army now advanced on Camulodunum (Colchester), Caratacus' capital. Only a token resistance was made, and Caratacus and his main army fled into Wales. It is thought that eleven kings of British tribes made a formal submission to Claudius who then left Britain and returned to Rome in triumph. The army in Britain now pushed forward.

The Twentieth Legion stayed in Colchester, the Second moved across the West Country, the Fourteenth advanced into the West Midlands, and the Ninth headed North. Its advance columns got as far as the River Humber.

Here the Ninth Legion, under the direction of Plautius, made a treaty with Aveon Cartimandua, whose lands stretched across most of Northern England where she ruled a confederation of tribes called the Brigantes. The Ninth Legion set up several bases, the two main ones being at Longthorpe near

Tombstone Of Valerius, Standard Bearer Of The Ninth Legion At Lincoln.

Peterborough. A little later they founded Lincoln which was to become one of the largest Roman cities in Britain. The exact date of these foundings is not clear but it is possible that Longthorpe was founded around 47 AD to 48 AD and Lincoln the following year 48 AD to 49 AD. In 47 AD a change of governor was made. His name was Publus Ostorius Scapula. This change of governorship brought swift attacks by the Britons, but Scapula put these down quickly and severely. It is thought that Longthorpe was established by the Ninth Legion after this British uprising.

Around this time Caratacus, who had been undertaking hit and run tactics against the Romans, made a fatal error. He committed his army to a pitched battle. He was defeated by the Fourteenth and Twentieth Legion and his wife, daughter and brother were captured.

Caratacus fled to Queen Cartimandua, although it seems more likely to her husband, a nobleman called Venutius, who was known to be anti-Roman. Cartimandua simply held Caratacus in captivity and informed the Romans who sent a detachment from the Ninth Legion to take Caratacus back in chains. He was eventually sent by Scapula to Rome where he so impressed the Emperor Claudius and the Senate that they gave him and his family their freedom. The situation in Britain continued to be turbulent.

Scapula died through ill health and a new governor was appointed, Aulus Didius Gallus. He had been successful in a campaign in southern Russia and decorated by the Emperor. Then in 54 AD the Emperor Claudius died. Circumstances were suspicious and it was widely thought that he was poisoned by his wife. Many of Claudius' good advisers fell from grace. Nero, the new Emperor, considered withdrawing from Britain for a time but did not as it would reflect badly on Claudius' previous military glories.

Back in Britain the Ninth Legion had sent envoys to Queen Cartimandua's court and, over the last few years, were well informed on the unrest in the North. In 56 AD Cartimandua took her husband Venutius' armour-bearer, a young man by the name of Vellocatus, as her lover. Venutius protested at the violation of their marriage. Cartimandua dismissed him from her court and Vellocatus became her consort. Venutius had a lot of support from other Celtic chiefs who were anti-Roman and they raised a large army. Meanwhile Cartimandua had seized her husband's family. The Romans sent a small force of auxiliaries which stopped Venutius' army but did not succeed in dispersing it. Gallus the new Governor was alarmed by these events and the Ninth Legion was mobilized and sent to help Cartimandua.

Caesius Nasica, the commander of the Ninth, defeated Venutius' army and saved Cartimandua from being overthrown, but it would appear that Venutius did at least end up controlling most of the Northern Region of Roman Britain. The Ninth Legion had to build more forts and one was to become the famous city of Lincoln.

In 60 AD King Prasutagus of the Iceni died, his kingdom being in the south-east of Britain. He left half of his large fortune to his two daughters and the other half to the Roman Emperor – but the Romans decided to obtain the whole of Prasutagus' wealth. The new Roman Governor, Caius Suetonius Paulinus, had taken most of the army into North Wales in a final attempt to break the power of the Druids. He had left Catus Decianus, the Chief Prosecutor, in charge during his absence. It was this greedy man who, with an army of veterans (many recently retired from the Ninth Legion but eager and brutal enough to seize a rich kingdom), attacked the Iceni court in an attempt to seize its wealth.

Understandably Prasutagus' widow, Queen Boudicca, protested at the pillaging of her court. Catus had the Queen stripped and whipped and her two daughters were found and raped by a group of drunken Roman soldiers.

In reprisal for these Roman attacks Queen Boudicca soon raised an army and marched on the colonial capital of the day Camulodunum (Colchester), where the perpetuators of her violation were stationed. The town was attacked and burnt to the ground. All men, women and children were put to death. Paulinus received a messenger from Camulodunum before it fell and left as soon as possible with his cavalry, instructing his infantry to follow. At the same time the Ninth Legion at Longthorpe received news of the attack.

The Legate of the Ninth was a man called Petillius Cerialis. His career was marked by the number of times he escaped from near military disasters and this remarkable achievement was to continue! Petillius Cerialis left with a force of 2,000 infantry and 500 cavalry. Boudicca's spies informed her of the movements of the Ninth Legion and she laid an ambush with 30,000 troops.

The Ninth were caught entirely by surprise and all 2,000 infantry were slaughtered. Petillius Cerialis just managed to escape with his cavalry back to Longthorpe.

Paulinus reached the River Dee. Part of his journey may have been made by ship. He took 500 cavalry and rode hard to London. Many of the richest merchants had fled in their boats to Gaul, as had Catus Decianus, the man who must ultimately be regarded as responsible for the whole uprising.

When Paulinus arrived in London the remaining people pleaded with him to defend them, but he knew with his limited cavalry it was impossible for him to do that. He advised the people leave London and go to Kent where the Celtic king was loyal to the Romans. Most did, so that when Boudicca's army arrived, very few were left; nevertheless she sacked and burned the city, slaying those who were.

In the meantime Paulinus was riding back down Watling Street to rejoin his army which he met somewhere in the Midlands. Boudicca sacked St Albans and was gathering even more forces. Paulinus had only about 10,000 troops remaining at his disposal.

Paulinus sent envoys to the Second Legion (Legio II *'Augusta'*) at Exeter but its commander, Poenius Postumus, refused to spare any men at all. It is not known if a request was made to the Ninth Legion at Longthorpe, but none of the Ninth Legion troops marched to help Paulinus. To be fair to the Ninth's Commander Petillius Cerialis, after the heavy defeat he suffered at the hands of Boudicca's army was in no real position to assist Paulinus.

The Roman army made camp near Lichfield. Paulinus had the whole of the Fourteenth Legion (Legio XIV *'Gemina'*) and some of the veterans of the Twentieth Legion (Legio XX *'Valeria'*). He also had auxiliaries collected from the towns sympathetic to the Romans that he had passed along the way.

When the two armies met, Boudicca's army was estimated to be over 100,000 men women and children. The Britons charged the Roman ranks and were met with a storm of javelins and arrows. Many Britons were slaughtered and they fell back to their wagons where the women and children were; however, these also were not spared by the advancing Romans. Enough Britons died to finish the rebellion for good. It is said that 80,000 died in this conflict including Queen Boudicca herself, and the site of this battle has never been satisfactorily identified to this day. How different British history may have been if the sheer force of numbers in Boudicca's army had overwhelmed the might and organization of Rome – but they failed.

Upon hearing of the British troubles the Emperor Nero immediately ordered an inquiry into the rebellion. In Britain Poenius Postumus, the commander of the second Legion, who had not given support, killed himself when he heard of

Paulinus' victory. The Ninth Legion then received 2,000 legionaries from the Rhine Legions which brought it back up to strength. Both the Second and the Ninth Legion joined Paulinus and carried out punitive measures against the Britons, many areas being laid waste. After this campaign the Ninth Legion now set about building up Lincoln, which was to be their new headquarters.

B) CONSOLIDATION:

In 68 AD the somewhat crazy reign of Nero ended as it had begun, in sudden death. The Senate had proclaimed the old general Galba Emperor and condemned Nero to death. A slave cut Nero's throat.

Galba was 73 years old and got off to a bad start by upsetting many people. Soon other would-be emperors emerged. In 69 AD the veteran troops in Germany, who had little loyalty to the Empire and even less to Galba, proclaimed Governor Vitellius Emperor. The Legions in Britain, including the Ninth, also supported Vitellius, but the Praetorian Guard proclaimed Otho as Emperor.

Rome now had three Emperors, Vitellius, Galba, and Otho! Within hours of the news of the other proclamations reaching Rome Galba was lured into the Forum and murdered by the Praetorian Guard leaving two Emperors, Otho and Vitellius.

Vitellius gathered his Rhine troops and marched south. He also ordered the British Legions to detach 2,000 troops from each and send them to his aid. Those Legions were the Second, Ninth, and Twentieth. These troops landed too late to take part in the Battle of Bedriacum, which ended in victory for Vitellius. When Otho heard the news of the defeat he took his own life. Vitellius was now Emperor by the time he reached Rome and his troops ran amok in the capital. Well has it been said that 'the Romans worst enemy were other Romans'!

The new Emperor very soon proved he was also unsuitable and was faced by a new challenge from the east. Legions in Egypt now proclaimed Vespasian as Emperor. Vespasian's forces moved quickly and met Vitellian forces near the site of the previous Battle of Bedriacum. The elements of the Ninth were in the centre formation but the battle was a crushing defeat for the Vitellian army and it is thought that most of the Ninth's troops were wiped out. The outcome of this battle was the storming of the Praetorian camp and Vitellius himself was killed by the mob. Vespasian, an able man at last, was now Emperor.

Meanwhile in Britain the extraordinary Petillius Cerialis, the old commander of the Ninth Legion, was made Governor of Britain replacing Vettius Bolanus, who had sent troops in support of Vitellius.

On arrival in Britain, Cerialis' main task was to deal with the threat on the Northern Frontier from the still restless Brigantian tribes, who at this time appear to be united behind Venutius their chief. Queen Cartimandua seems to have either died or gone into exile some time before. Cerialis brought over a new Legion, the II 'Adiutrix', only recently formed from marines and intended as a reserve Legion in Britain. This Legion was moved into Lincoln. Cerialis then ordered his second-in-command, Julius Agricola, to advance in the North West with the Twentieth Legion while he advanced out of Lincoln with his best Legion, the Ninth.

Venutius had for some time been building massive fortifications at Stanwick in North Yorkshire. Cerialis knew this and decided to consolidate his own position first. His scouts reported a good site for his headquarters where two rivers met near hilly ground with a large forest surrounding the area. Here the Ninth Legion founded York in 71 AD and here they could be supplied by sea if need be. The fortress was built on the north side of what is now the river Ouse, and the river Foss joined the Ouse on the east side of the fort. The name of this fort was

'Eboracum' – known today as York.

From York the Ninth Legion struck out and defeated the Brigantian forces in two major battles, one near Moulton and another near the River Humber. The Ninth then built many smaller forts and, on the western shores of Britain, Agricola had reached the area of Carlisle. Brigantian forces were now cut off from their supply routes from the south, the west, and the east. Only northern supply lines remained open but units of the Ninth Legion joined up with units of the Twentieth Legion in the Stanmore Pass and soon Stanwick was cut off from all lines of supply and communication. Venetius had no choice, now he would have to come out and fight.

Cerialis and Agricola would not have attacked Stanwick directly; however, it is not known where the final battle with Venutius took place except that it may be Venutius tried a break-out from Stanwick to the north, or may have even tried to go for York itself! Whatever happened he disappears from the pages of history about 73 AD almost certainly after a major battle which ended in his defeat. For the time being the Northern Frontier was peaceful.

Cerialis was recalled to Rome in 74 AD and replaced by Julius Fortinus who then campaigned in Wales with three Legions while the Ninth was left to guard the Northern Frontier and build up York as a major fort. In 77 AD Fortinus was replaced by Julius Agricola. This man had been Cerialis' second-in-command and commanded the Twentieth Legion who had fought alongside the Ninth.

Agricola struck at once into Wales and permanently conquered Anglesey. The following year Agricola consolidated his position in the North. Many of the smaller tribes surrendered to the Romans, but the threat from much larger tribes in Caledonia (Scotland) continued. In 79 AD York's defences were strengthened and a new earth bank built, new timbers replaced old, and the ditch work around the fortress doubled.

C) SCOTLAND:

In the following year, 80 AD, Agricola struck north with the Twentieth Legion from Chester in the west and the Ninth Legion from York in the east. The Twentieth were building up Carlisle as a forward base and the Ninth made their forward base at Corbridge on the River Tyne, there they could be supplied from York by land and sea.

Vespasian died in 79 AD whilst Agricola was campaigning. Vespasian was succeeded as Emperor by his son Titus who was a good man but died in 81 AD. He was succeeded in turn by Domitian his brother, who was universally suspected of poisoning Titus and became a cruel and unpopular Emperor. However, he does not appear to have interfered with Agricola's campaigns in Scotland.

The years 81 AD and 82 AD were used by Agricola to consolidate the gains he had made in previous years. The Ninth Legion built many small forts in east Britain, as did the Twentieth in the west. In 82 AD Agricola meditated long and hard upon an attack on Ireland, though it is just as well for his reputation that it was never attempted.

Agricola had sheltered one of the Irish kings who had been expelled in civil strife. He was kept at hand in friendly guise to see if an opportunity to invade ever arose but the King told Agricola that Ireland could be conquered with just one Legion! The Ninth had been put on alert for this campaign but treachery was always suspected and the idea was dropped. Instead the next year 83 AD Agricola advanced north of the Forth. His western army was to be supplied by sea from Chester.

The Ninth Legion was used as the initial spearhead in the east and somewhere north of the Forth they made camp. The Roman army was advancing in seven columns. The Ninth was divided from the main army so the Britons concentrated their army together and prepared for a night attack. By 11 o'clock most of the Ninth Legion had turned in and it is thought that the Britons attacked soon after. The alert was sounded but troops on the watch were overrun and a massacre only averted by the late arrival of Agricola with the rest of the army. The Britons melted back into the night.

The Ninth had lost a considerable number of men. This was a disaster, perhaps a lesson that remained unlearned and an example of things to come for the Ninth for after this they became known as 'The Unlucky Ninth' because this was the second time disaster had befallen them during the British invasion, the first being the loss of 2,000 men at the hands of Boudicca's army. At the end of 83 AD Agricola wintered by the River Tay and built up supplies. He is also thought to have received reinforcement auxiliaries, many from southern Britain.

With the harsh northern winter behind them in the summer of 84 AD, and with the support of the Roman fleet, Agricola advanced again in two columns, the Twentieth Legion heading one, and the Ninth Legion the other. At last these two columns forced a large army of 30,000 Britons, under the leadership of a Caledonian Chief called Calgacus, to battle.

Agricola kept his two Legions in reserve and instead used his auxiliary infantry of about 8,000 men supported by 5,000 auxiliary cavalry. The Britons held the high ground with a large number of chariots in front of British foot soldiers.

The Romans attacked the chariots with cavalry backed up by a hail of javelins and arrows from the infantry and the whole British line crumbled when the Roman cavalry swept round and began attacking from the rear. In this chaos the British lost over 10,000 men. Roman losses were about 350 men; the Ninth Legion lost no men and took little or no part in the battle which became known as the Battle of Mons Graupius. Despite this it was to be the last recorded historic battle in which the Ninth Legion took part.

Lorica Armour From Newstead, Scotland, Late First Century AD.

With 20,000 men escaping from the Battle of Mons Graupius it meant that Agricola would face more hostilities in the future and Roman scouts could find no trace of them! A massive concentration of Roman garrisons were now established in the northern reaches of Scotland. During the winter Agricola sent a fleet round the coast to prove Britain was indeed an island and the Ninth Legion returned to York to reform. Whilst all this was going on the question of Ireland came up again. Could Ireland be conquered?

D) IRELAND:

By the spring of 85 AD the Ninth Legion had completed its refit and stood ready to campaign in Ireland if required to do so. Agricola sent over a Roman contingent to a friendly Irish king but once again he was put off the idea as officers of the Ninth Legion informed him that Ireland was made up of small but very strong kingdoms, often at war with each other.

He did, however, set up a trading post at Drumanagh, 15 miles north of the present day city of Dublin, with the intention of monitoring activities in Ireland. The Romans would now be able to act if the troubles in Ireland weakened its petty kings or threatened Roman Britain. Drumanagh would later be turned into a large 40 acre fort with a string of Roman villas along the Irish Sea coast. Meanwhile the known history of the Ninth Legion almost entirely disappears into the mists of time.

Only two tombstones belonging to men of the Ninth Legion have so far been found in York. One is of a soldier from Northern Italy but his name is unknown as the tombstone is incomplete. The other, which can be seen in the Yorkshire Museum, is of the Ninth Legion's Standard Bearer Lucius Ducius Rufinus. An inscription to Silvanus, the god of the woods, made by the Ninth Legion's 'Clerk' Celerinius has also been found. Here the mystery of the Ninth Legion's whereabouts begins in earnest.

It is thought that a detachment of the Ninth Legion, probably three cohorts, served in the war against the Chatts in 83 AD commanded by a tribune called Laticlavius.

During Domitian's reign as Emperor, Agricola returned to Rome in 85 AD and Domitian is thought to have poisoned this great man soon afterwards, viewing him as a threat. Agricola's governorship of Britain was then handed over to Sallustius Lucullus who was, in turn, executed by Domitian in 90 AD for naming his new lance after him!

In 96 AD Domitian was murdered by a steward called Stephanus and a Roman lawyer called Nerva was elected as Emperor. Nerva was over 60 years old at the time, died in 98 AD, and was succeeded by Trajan, a soldier whose popularity with the troops was never in doubt. A stable leader at last, Trajan was to extend the Empire further than it had ever been stretched before.

Back in Britain the last known evidence of the Ninth Legion's existence was being recorded on a gate's commemorative inscription at York which was found in King's Square dedicated to Trajan. The Ninth Legion is referred to in the last line of this inscription and the date would be around 107 AD to 108 AD.

Extensive work was done at York during this time. Stone buildings had now been built including the Legion's headquarters and bathhouse. The southern wall was rebuilt of stone from a quarry where Bradford now stands. Historians are generally undecided exactly how much of York was rebuilt in stone during this period but, by January 109 AD, all building work in this phase had probably been completed. No real evidence after this date for the existence of the Ninth Legion has yet been found.

XVI

THEORETICAL HISTORY OF THE NINTH LEGION AFTER 108 AD

This chapter deals with what may have happened to the Ninth Legion after the rebuilding of York in 107-108 AD, for no real evidence of the Ninth Legion after this date has ever been found. Only historical theories have been put forward and they seem to keep changing as new discoveries are made and new ideas about Roman history rise to prominence. All the established theories and current new theories are detailed in this chapter with arguments for and against dealt with in the following chapters.

THEORY I – THE CHEVIOT HILLS:

By the beginning of 109 AD all the rebuilding had been completed in York but the Northern lands were still very hostile to Roman rule. Emperor Trajan was expanding the Empire, Legions were always on the move (or at least parts of them) and, in 110 AD, two cohorts of the Ninth Legion were transferred to Nijmegen (now in Holland) on the German border. This was thought safe as any trouble could be contained in Britain using less troops, but in 115 AD the Northern tribes struck back hard and burnt many small forts including Malton only 20 miles from York.

The Ninth Legion now had three hard years fighting until the situation was calm again. However, Roman troops in Scotland had been cut off and only forts on the River Tay could be supplied, and that was by sea. Governor Pompeius Falco decided to relieve these forts but, whilst this was still being planned, Emperor Trajan died in 117 AD and Hadrian took over.

This was not sufficient to stop the Ninth's final fateful expedition North.

By spring 118 AD York was filled by a further 6,000 auxiliary troops. In the first week of May that year an army group, including most of the Ninth Legion and its auxiliaries and cavalry, moved out of York and headed North with the troops in the Tay forts expecting them. As the 10,000 men left York, spies from the local tribes informed their chiefs, who in turn informed the Scottish tribes of the Ninth's advance north. At first there was little resistance, tribes submitted, but it was noted that there was a general lack of able-bodied men in these camps!

The chiefs of the Scottish tribes gathered as many men together as they could muster, possibly numbering over 30,000 foot soldiers, 1,000 chariots, plus many horsemen – but then where to attack the Roman army? It was remembered many years before that the Ninth Legion had almost been wiped out during a night attack so it was decided to try this method again. As the Ninth Legion headed north they travelled over the Cheviot Hills keeping to the high ground. In the undulating lowland areas lay large tracts of forest in which thousands of the Northern tribesmen hid.

The Romans had to make camp and they dug the usual defences which were heavily guarded. By the time most of the camp had turned in, the tribesmen attacked from one side with 5,000 men and broke through into the camp.

Then two other attacks came with 10,000 men and the camp was almost overrun completely, the Ninth Legion just managing to construct some sort of defensive line. By the morning the whole camp was completely surrounded with all cavalry horses lost or taken.

An order to 'break out' was given and those Legionaries who managed this monumental achievement found other groups of tribesmen waiting for them and were slaughtered where they stood. On the further hills chariots and horsemen rode down any surviving Romans. By the end of the day every single man of the Ninth Legion and their auxiliaries had been slain.

Northern tribal leaders then gave orders that no evidence of the Ninth Legion was to remain. All bodies were stripped and burnt and the ashes buried or scattered. All cursed Roman weapons were to be melted down and destroyed which did cause some trouble as the tribesmen valued these highly, but the order was nevertheless carried out. All efforts to find the Ninth's Golden Eagle failed. The Legion's Standard Bearer had hidden it and it has never been found – it still lies somewhere hidden in the Cheviot Hills.

Meanwhile the forts on the Tay waited for the Ninth Legion and at first when there was no sign of them it created no cause for concern. Delays were common. A ship from York arrived and the sailors were very surprised that the Ninth had not yet turned up! Other ships came and went carrying news that the Ninth had gone missing. When the Tribune left in charge of York heard such tales and sent out horsemen nothing was found. Even the forward camp had not heard or seen anything of the Ninth.

The Governor was informed and he sent 5,000 auxiliaries to York. In support the Twentieth Legion at Chester sent five cohorts to the Border. Carlisle was reinforced. A messenger was sent to the Emperor Hadrian in Rome who was most concerned and put an 'oath of silence' on the news of the Ninth's disappearance fearing instability in the Roman ranks.

Hadrian then considered the problem in Britain very seriously and came over (in what year it is not known for certain though it is thought perhaps to be 122 AD, but possibly as early as 119 AD). He brought with him the Sixth Legion, Legio VI 'Victris', and made his headquarters at York. Those remaining soldiers of the Ninth Legion there were incorporated into the Sixth Legion. Hadrian then withdrew all Roman forces from Scotland and Ireland and built his famous wall from Wallsend-on-Tyne to Bowness-on-Solway, a distance of 80 Roman miles (73 English miles). Three Legions built it, the II 'Augusta', VI 'Victris', and XX 'Valeria' – perhaps a fitting tribute to what was once Rome's finest Legion, the 'Glorious Ninth'?

There is probably more circumstantial evidence to support this theory than any other.

THEORY II – THE SOLWAY FIRTH:

However, some think the Ninth Legion actually assisted in building the wall and survived independently to endure further adventures.

After restoring order in the north between 114 AD and 117 AD, it was decided by the new Emperor Hadrian that the Ninth Legion would be moved to Carlisle and another Legion, the Sixth Legion, would move to York. So, in 118 AD, the Ninth moved to Carlisle. It was here that they were to have built a large fort like they did initially at York, but in 119 AD trouble in the north started again and the Roman forts in Scotland, which had been relieved, were once again cut off. It was now decided on another two-pronged advance into Scotland.

This time the Sixth Legion drove north from York and the Ninth Legion from Carlisle. When the Ninth reached the Solway Firth they camped on the south side. In the morning they started to cross. The Commander, not knowing the sands and taking this route in order to save time, ran into trouble with the ground and was then heavily attacked by the northern tribesmen from the north bank. The Ninth Legion was forced to retreat back across the Solway Firth and right into the tide and soft sands. Here they perished and sank into the oncoming tide and quicksands, leaving no trace whatsoever.

An unlikely theory but just as possible as the previous one based on the lack of concrete evidence.

THEORY III - RANNOCH MOOR:

Rewind the story slightly for the next instalment:

After subduing the uprising in North Yorkshire in 115 AD, the Ninth Legion was ordered by Governor Pompeius Falco to relieve the forts on the River Tay that were still cut off and, in the summer of 117 AD, the Ninth Legion finally reached these Roman forts. All opposition had been dealt with on the way up and, having been very successful, the Legion's Commander decided to continue this policy and destroy the surrounding tribes. Taking a large force of 12,000 to 15,000 men, he set off the following year to campaign in central and northern Scotland; however, he made a fatal tactical mistake and split his forces, the idea being to trap a large group of tribal warriors thought to be gathering in the area of Loch Rannock in Perthshire.

The main body of the Ninth with auxiliaries came up from

the south and were attacked by 5,000 Scottish tribesmen. The Legion formed squares and for a time held out, but the second body of the Roman army were unable to reach this main Roman force now surrounded on Rannoch Moor. As more tribesmen reinforcements arrived the Ninth Legion was cut down and none survived. As a result Hadrian withdrew all Roman forces from Scotland and built phase one of his now famous wall beginning in 118 AD.

Apparently today local people still talk of the Ninth Legion as being lost on Rannoch Moor.

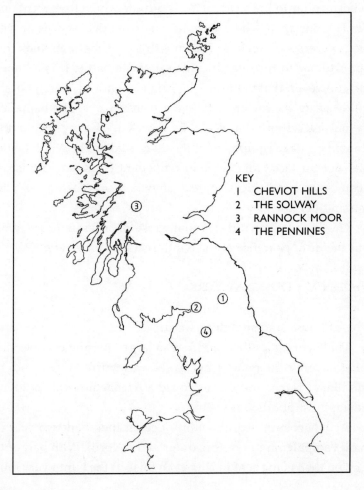

KEY
1 CHEVIOT HILLS
2 THE SOLWAY
3 RANNOCK MOOR
4 THE PENNINES

THEORY IV – THE PENNINES:

After the British tribal uprising of 115 AD the Ninth Legion restored peace. But in 117 AD another large tribal uprising spread through what is now south Yorkshire and Lancashire. Communications were cut from London and Chester. Governor Falco ordered the Twentieth Legion based at Chester and the Ninth Legion based at York to deal with this uprising and restore communications.

The Ninth Legion marched to attack a large group of hostile tribesmen far to the south of York, a route which took them over the Pennine road where they were surrounded and destroyed. No soldiers survived and again British tribesmen took this opportunity to remove all evidence of the battle. It is a known fact, however, that battles in the past were always automatically followed by the victors sending scavengers over the battlefield to loot everything that could be recycled. The mystery is that Roman military equipment of the kind used by the Ninth Legion has not surfaced in any unusual quantity in any British or Scottish archaeological context anywhere associated with the missing Legion.

The Sixth Legion did eventually restore order in these regions but the disappearance of the Ninth remains a mystery.

THEORY V – DEFEAT AT YORK:

This is simple and straightforward.

The theory goes that in 115 AD a large uprising occurred and Malton, only 20 miles from York, was burnt down and the auxiliary force there destroyed. Archaeological evidence generally supports this event.

As has been noted, the Ninth Legion then had two years of hard campaigning to restore order in the North. With part of the Legion then being sent to Nijmegen this left the Ninth very much under-strength and British tribes in the North saw this and decided to attack York directly. It was planned for early 118 AD and a night attack thought to be the ideal strategy. One cold February night when the moon was full, over 20,000 tribesmen stormed York.

Military action during the bitter winter months was entirely unexpected and caught the Romans off guard. The attack was well co-ordinated and local tribesmen knew the defences of the city well. The walls were soon overrun and the main barracks attacked with full force. Very few soldiers were able to defend themselves trapped inside the barracks, and the cold seriously affected the Legionaries' performance once outside. By morning all of the Ninth Legion was destroyed, along with the Roman city of York.

This theory is almost impossible to substantiate based on archaeological remains. If York was overrun then the conquerors almost certainly chose to retain the city without creating the distinctive evidence associated with burning structures. It looks like the fort simply remained to be taken back at some future date and put back into full service later in that century by the Roman army.

There is just one possibility – that the superstitious Britons chose not to use the city structures at all and simply left after their victory, leaving the non-military remains of the Roman inhabitants to continue and rebuild.

THEORY VI – DEATH AT SEA:

The uprising of 115 AD was decisively put down by the Ninth Legion and, by about 118 AD, a peaceful normality had returned.

The Governor of Britain, Pompeius Falco, ordered the Ninth Legion to force open a passage to the forts on the River Tay, but it was found by reconnaissance that a much larger force than one Legion would be needed to achieve this. The Commander of the Ninth decided to request and await reinforcements but, before any such forces arrived, a ship docked from the forts with news that immediate forces were needed in order to hold them. Now the only way remaining to successfully do this was by sea.

A large part of the Ninth Legion, who were used to marine action from past campaigns, hastily boarded on to whatever ships could be commandeered or built at short notice and set sail for the Tay. On this fateful voyage a sudden storm arose and all ships were lost out at sea with no survivors from the Legion or crews.

A somewhat unlikely scenario but one theory nonetheless.

THEORY VII – REASSIGNMENT:

During the start of Hadrian's rule the Ninth Legion had been ordered to put down a rising somewhere in the North, possibly as already outlined. The Legion left York in 118 AD and was very badly defeated in a battle where many soldiers fled.

Hadrian then came over with the Sixth Legion and, being a strict disciplinarian, cashiered the whole Ninth Legion, with Staff Officers being transferred to the Sixth Legion and, perhaps, many of the disgraced soldiers and auxiliaries being sent to help construct Hadrian's Wall.

This makes the Ninth Legion simply vanish into Hadrian's other Legions without the embarrassing facts being recorded.

THEORY VIII – IRELAND:

This theory goes that, in 85 AD to 86 AD, a trading post was set up in Ireland by the Ninth Legion where present day Drumanagh now stands. This later became a strong fort. Other small forts were set up along the coast, one where present day Dublin now stands; this being only 15 miles from the main Roman fort at

Drumanagh.

By about 107 AD Rome occupied much of the west coast of Ireland. The Romans had also breached up to 30 miles inland and now controlled at least two of the coastal kingdoms, but the country was always highly volatile; some kingdoms were friendly others were not. The Ninth Legion was about to be moved to Carlisle from York where another Legion was due to be posted; however, events in Ireland changed all that.

Roman forts in Ireland were under threat due to new kings who did not want the Romans on Irish soil. The Ninth Legion was sent back to the now 40 acre fort at Drumanagh. Once settled in they began a series of punitive strikes against the troublesome kings in the west.

All went well at first, then in 120 AD a large military expedition left Drumanagh to campaign against the kingdoms in the west and that was the last anyone ever saw of the Ninth Legion. In haste Emperor Hadrian withdrew all Roman forces from Ireland. The Irish petty kings then systematically destroyed all evidence of Roman occupation. No records of the event were kept and, even years later, archaeologists and the National Museum of Ireland keep this great historical secret from the world.

This theory may well be the right one. Conspiracy and hidden evidence?

Now let's move the clock forward to look at other possibilities for the eventual fate of the Ninth Legion beyond these islands.

THEORY IX – THE JEWISH WAR:

In 120 AD Emperor Hadrian came to Britain. He bought with him the Sixth Legion, Legio VI 'Victrix', from the Lower Rhine. The entire Ninth Legion at York was then transferred to Nijmegen (now in Holland) as the Legion had suffered heavy casualties in the summer of 117 AD and had problems with discipline ever since. The Ninth Legion was then reformed and trained up.

Twelve years later, in 132 AD, this much improved Legion

was transferred to take part in the Jewish War. The Roman Commander Sextus Juilus Severus was transferred from Britain to take command in the East and, on his way, he collected the Ninth Legion; and it was during this war that the Ninth once again suffered heavy losses. This time Antonnius Pius disbanded the Legion in 153 AD.

A possibility.

THEORY X – THE PARTHIAN WAR:

Continuing further along the path of Roman history this theory goes that, after taking part in the Jewish War in 132 AD, the Ninth Legion returned to Nijmegen.

In 161 AD the Parthians started another war and the Ninth Legion was quickly dispatched to the East to stem the Parthian assault. The commander of the Ninth Legion, a man called Severianus, made his headquarters at Elegeia.

From Elegeia, Severianus marched the Ninth further east where he was attacked and surrounded by horse archers with powerful composite bows. The whole Legion was destroyed and never reformed.

This is the latest theory and the one currently most favoured by experts.

THEORY XI – PLAGUE IN THE EAST:

As previously, in 161 AD the Ninth Legion was ordered to Parthia to stop the massive Parthian advance. The Parthian army was defeated by the Romans under Severianus and, in 165 AD, the Parthian capital Ctesiphon was placed under siege by Roman forces and fell. It is said that the troops of the Ninth Legion burnt down the Royal Palace.

Ctesiphon, now under Roman control, was to be made the base for a conquering drive even further east with the Ninth Legion forming the spearhead of the campaign. Then a plague of some kind broke out and most of the Ninth Legion died and the Roman troops were forced to withdraw. After this the Ninth Legion was disbanded and those who survived incorporated into the Thirtieth Legion.

Frankly not very likely.

THEORY XII – CHINA:

This is the last theory, without doubt the least likely, and centres around a Roman city in China, how this city came to be, and the involvement of the Ninth Legion.

In 53 BC, whilst the Ninth Legion was with Julius Caesar in Gaul, the new Proconsul of Syria, a very ambitious man called Marcus Lincinius Crassus was given command of the army in the East and prepared to undertake a series of campaigns that would equal Alexandra the Great. This vain man was to find a place in the English Dictionary: *Crass, i.e. grossly stupid*, for Crassus was about to lead the armies of the East to total destruction in one of the most incompetently led campaigns in military history.

First Crassus crossed the Euphrates in 53 BC. Several Mesopotamian cities gave him allegiance which he then garrisoned. The city of Zenodotia resisted and was destroyed and Crassus then wintered in Syria.

The next spring Crassus massed seven Legions, 5,000 auxiliary infantrymen, and about the same number of cavalry. His son arrived from Southern Gaul with 1,000 Gallic cavalrymen. Some time later King Artavasdes of Armenia arrived with a small army of about 6,000 troops and a promise of a further 40,000 more. The King then advised Crassus to attack Parthia through the southern foothills of Armenia as the Parthians, who were very strong in cavalry, would have difficulty in operating freely there and the region was well watered.

Despite this good local advice Crassus decided to take the shorter and more direct route through the desert into Parthia and crossed the Euphrates during a bad storm. The superstitious Romans thought this to be a bad omen and they were right!

To add insult to injury Crassus was then tricked by an Arab chieftain called Ariamnes who told him to hasten after the Parthian army which was, at that very moment, retreating across the desert. Fatally Crassus decided to allow the devious Arabs to lead his army in pursuit of these Parthians.

Meanwhile Orodes II, King of the Parthians, split his real army in two. Orodes led one part of the army into Armenia and started to pillage the country, the second part of the army he gave to his best general, a man of great leadership named Surenas, whose task was to slow down the Roman army until Orodes could rejoin him after the raid on Armenia.

The Romans headed into the desert and the Arabs then rode away. King Artavasdes could not send his 40,000 troops to help Crassus as they were needed to stop Orodes II from further sacking Armenia. Crassus was strongly advised by his Generals to either rejoin King Artavasdes in Armenia, or to take the easier route through the foothills. Crassus ignored this advice and, instead, carried on into the desert!

As his army drew nearer to the ancient town of Carrhae, riders from the advance column told Crassus that a large body of

Parthian cavalry horse archers were advancing towards his army. They soon appeared and surrounded the Romans and kept up a deadly stream of arrows from their composite bows. The Romans had expected Parthian cataphracts in complete armour but, although these heavily armoured cavalry knights were seen, they were held back in favour of the fast striking archers and refused to engage the Romans. The Parthians brought up camels with spare quivers of arrows so their bows were always kept supplied even in the desert.

The Romans made a determined charge with cavalry under Publius, Crassus' son, but they were surrounded on a hill nearby and wiped out. The Legionaries formed a square called a 'testudo' but many arrows got below and through the shields and wounded hundreds of foot soldiers. By nightfall 20,000 Romans has been killed and Crassus was dead in the shifting sands. Only one quarter of the Roman army managed to escape back to Syria. 10,000 were taken prisoner, moved to Margiana, and offered their lives if they formed into groups to help defend Parthia's eastern border. This they did.

Some Romans escaped to become mercenaries for other rulers. Romans even went further to the Chinese who welcomed these brave soldiers who would be able to guard their frontier. Eventually the Chinese allowed these men to build a frontier city called Li-gien. From this city Roman military influence was then recorded in China. Eventually the city of Li-gien was destroyed by the Tibetans who overran the whole area in 746 AD but the Romans knew of the existence of this city some years after Crassus' military disaster at Carrhae.

The story goes that when the Romans overran the Parthian capital Ctesiphon in 165 AD further evidence of the Roman city of Li-gien came to light. It was decided by some to press on and find this city so the Roman Commander chose the Ninth Legion. The Ninth set out in the summer of 165 AD from Ctesiphon to reach the Roman city of Li-gien and disappeared.

A very unlikely theory but Li-gien did actually exist and there is strong evidence of Roman's being there at some point in its history.

By 169 AD the Ninth Legion was no longer on the Roman army lists and, further more, no trace or knowledge of its fate during the preceding 61 years has yet been found.

XVII

CONCLUSIONS

No matter what the 'theory' the last known hard evidence of the Ninth Legion was left in 108 AD when the Legion rebuilt a large part of York so it is here that we should begin to reach our conclusions.

In 115 AD there was widespread unrest and a very serious revolt of the Northern tribes, many of the settlements and forts which were manned by auxiliaries were destroyed, Ilkeley was burnt down, Malton (only 20 miles from York) was overrun and destroyed despite being a fort which covered 22 acres, and it is certain that there were heavy losses. In fact it was very likely that the whole garrison of Malton was wiped out to a man!

This would give some credence to the theory that the same fate happened to the Ninth Legion at York, but the 'York Archaeological Trust' have stated that there has been no evidence that York was ever destroyed during this period of Roman occupation, and the 'war dead' from Malton also remain 'missing in action'.

During this revolt the Ninth Legion must have seen much fighting and may have been under siege in York for a short time. A theory that this may have happened was put forward in the 1920's but, in view of what the Archaeological Trust has said and the evidence on the ground, the theory that the Ninth Legion was

Roman Sewer Under Church St. York.

York Archaeological Trust

wiped out whilst in York itself can almost certainly be eliminated. York also shows no evidence of ever being 'sacked'!

The popular theory that the Ninth Legion 'disappeared round about this time on a military expedition in an unrecorded battle in which they were massacred to a man' has now been disputed by modern historians, who have suggested that the Ninth was, in fact, simply transferred to Nijmegen. They suggest at Nijmegen the Legion refitted and then, as the theories have outlined, may have seen service in the Jewish War of 130 AD to 135 AD. They go on to say that the Ninth was involved in the Parthian War in 161 AD and identify it as the Legion destroyed by Vologaesus in this war. But another Legion, the Twenty Second XXII *'Deioteriana'*, seems more likely to be the Legion wiped out in the Parthian War not the IX *'Hispana'* ! If this is the case then we are still left asking the question: 'What did happen to the Ninth?'

Historical evidence of Roman military disasters of this time can be found in a letter written by a man from North Africa called Fronto who was a tutor to Emperor Marcus Aurelius. He wrote to his former pupil during the time of the Parthian War of 161 AD to 165 AD on hearing the terrible news that Severianus Maximum and a whole Legion with a great many auxiliaries had been massacred.

In his letter Fronto made the following comment to the Emperor regarding a previous great military disaster which was evidently still fresh in his mind: *"Again in the reign of your grandfather Hadrian, what a slaughter of soldiers was made by the Jews and what a slaughter by the Britons."*

This reference to the slaughter of Roman soldiers 'by the Britons' can only mean a first-class catastrophe had occurred at some point during the reign of Hadrian. The nature and extent of this great disaster in Britain could have been the overwhelming destruction and extinction of the Ninth Legion,

Legio IX *'Hispana'*, from the garrison of Eboracum (York) in about the years 118 AD to 120 AD. This is possibly the best supporting evidence for a military disaster of this kind.

At the beginning of the eighteenth century there appeared another possible clue as to what may have happened to the Ninth. A tile was found in Micklegate, York, and used by a bell founder as part of the brickwork around his moulds. The discovery of this possibly misleading tile fragment was made by a Mr Smith who had a foundry making bells around 1707. The one very much defaced tile, now lost, was reputed to have the inscription 'LEGIO IX VICTRIX' on it, giving rise to a theory that the Ninth Legion was in some later period resurrected as a new Legion, Legio IX *'Victrix'*. This theory is considered extremely dubious as the tile has disappeared and, in view of its defaced condition noted at the time, it would be unwise to consider it as evidence that the Ninth Legion was reformed at York, perhaps after heavy losses.

Another story, which would appear to be almost as dubious, is of a coin of Carausius, which now cannot be traced. The coin apparently had inscribed on it 'Leg VIIII GE'. It is quite certain that there was only ever one 'Ninth Legion' and only with the amalgamation of another 'Ninth Legion' could the term *'Gemina'* (GE) be applied. The probable explanation is that the person who found the coin misread 'X' for 'V' and there were 'Leg XIII Gem' and 'Leg XIIII Gem' stationed on the continent at various times.

XVIII

THE HARD EVIDENCE

If the Ninth Legion was lost whilst based at York can we be more specific as to when this may have possibly occurred? The answer is yes.

It has been shown by the inscription found on what was once the site of a gate in King's Square that this stone gate was built in the 11th year of Trajan's reign which was 108 AD to 109 AD, and material is available to show that Legio VI 'Victrix', the Sixth Legion, arrived in Britain before 123 AD.

Therefore the Ninth Legion in Britain was destroyed, disappeared, moved away, or disbanded at some point in the 14 years between these two dates.

Fronto's reference to the slaughter of Roman troops in Britain having occurred in the *"reign of Hadrian"* probably reduces the period further to 117 AD to 123 AD, and there has not been found any reference at all to warlike operations during Hadrian's stay in Britain which occurred in or around 120 AD to 121 AD.

It is generally thought among experts that the new Legion, the Sixth, had preceded the Emperor Hadrian and crushed a revolt of some kind. This would place the arrival of the Sixth Legion early in 120 AD after winter had subsided, during which time conflicts were usually avoided if at all possible.

That reduces the real possibility that the Ninth Legion were no more at some point during the three years between the spring of 117 AD and the onset of winter 119 AD. Something happened to them in the years AD 117, 118, or 119. Can we then narrow this time-window even further?

The following inscription at the base of a statue found at Minturnae in Italy was erected to the memory of Lucius

Burbuleius Octatus Ligarianus, one of the most distinguished officials of the Antonine period around 144 AD to 145 AD. The translated inscription reads as follows: *"To Lucius Burbuleius, son of Lucius, of the Quirinan tribe, Octatus Ligaran Consul, Augustus Pius in which office he died. Under the same Emperor and the late Emperor Hadrian Governor of Cappadocia, Curator of Public Works, Prefect of the Treasury, Pro Consol of Sicily, Legatus of Syria, Legatus of Legio XVI, Flavia Firma Commissioner of Narbo, Ancona and Tarracina, Curator of the Claudian Cassian and Ciminian Ways, Praetor Aedile Quaestor of Pontus and Bithynia,* **Tribunus Laticlarius in Legio IX "Hispana",** *Police Magistrate Patron of the Colony. (Minturae). This monument is erected by the pious care of Rasina, the nurse of his daughters."*

The most important and vital point of this inscription is that Ligarianus was Governor of Cappadocia in 138 AD, possibly assuming that office the preceding year. There is written evidence that the career of Ligarianus followed almost exactly the same lines as that of Agricola who took eighteen years to rise from the lowest level of the official ladder to a Governorship – in his case that of Britain. Taking this into account, Ligarianus' career could only have started at the very earliest in 117 AD to 118 AD. His first promotion to *"Tribune in the Ninth Legion"* would not, therefore, have occurred before 118 AD and, in that case, the Legio IX *'Hispana'* would still have been in existence in that year.

The least service for a Tribune would be a year so the Ninth Legion would therefore still be in York in 118 AD and into 119 AD.

Some will say that this evidence will give some strength to the argument that the Ninth Legion may have been transferred – but does it? If the Ninth Legion had been destroyed in Scotland when it left York a Tribune would have been left in charge of York. Could that Tribune have been Lucius Ligerianus? It could have been possible as he was very young and not experienced in warfare. The most experienced Tribunes would have been needed with the main part of the Legion.

As winter gave way to spring in 119 AD, did a large force of British or Caledonian (Pictish) warriors rise up and descend upon York, drawing out the Ninth Legion to its doom? Was the Roman city of Eburacum left desolate apart from its Tribune, women and children, for a year until the Legio VI *'Victrix'*, the Sixth Legion, arrived in 120 AD to relieve them?

However, some claim the Ninth Legion was not destroyed at this time – so what of those other fates that could have befallen them?

As has already been noted, recent evidence has come to light that the Romans did in fact land in Ireland and set up a trading post on the east coast at Drumanagh. This then built up into a large fort and it could be that the Ninth Legion helped in the building of this, in constructing the first roads and establishing some small villas and settlements along the east coast.

Coins found on the fort site are no later than the Emperor Hadrian's reign, probably from the same time Scotland was evacuated by the Romans anticipating construction of Hadrian's Wall. Could it be possible that the Ninth Legion, who were perhaps eventually going to transfer to Carlisle, went to Ireland in the 120's only to be destroyed whilst trying to expand Roman rule in that country ? This theory is rather unlikely but would conveniently answer the mystery of the complete disappearance of the Legion followed by no further reference to it.

At the time of writing very little information is coming out of Ireland and Irish historians are disagreeing as to the extent of the Roman occupation. Although there is yet no direct evidence of the destruction of the Ninth in Ireland, there is other material which, in spite of its indirectness, is of a most important character as it points to a date for the survival of the Legion after the accession of Hadrian.

In the early 1960's, a journal was published which raised a

possibility that the Ninth Legion survived after 120 AD. This came from a set of parchments found in a cave in Palestine. These documents relate to three Provincial Governors of Arabia, Julius Julianus in 125 AD, Aninius Sextius Floretinus in 127 AD, and Hector Herpos in 130 AD.

Florentinus, Governor in 127 AD, was already known as a monument to him had been found in Petra which tells of his career before he was Governor of Arabia. He had been the Proconsul of Narbonensis (modern day Provence), before that he had been *'Legate of IX Hispana'* – but the date of this is not known – or is it? Historians have pointed out that Florentinus would have been the Legate commanding the Ninth after 120 AD unless he had been a Proconsul for at least ten years, which is not very likely. In all probability he should have been the Legate of the Ninth Legion from about 120 AD to 124 AD.

Despite this calculation it has been known for Roman stone masons to make errors on monuments; however, there remains the possibility that Floretinus might well have been sent by Emperor Hadrian to rebuild the Ninth Legion after most of it had been lost somewhere in England, Scotland, or Ireland, after the year 119 AD.

Further evidence of other officers that were in the Ninth Legion has also been found which casts doubt on the end of the Legion being in the year 119 AD.

Aemilius Carrs and Novius Crispinus were known to have served in the Ninth Legion, in the case of Aemilius probably during Trajan's time as Emperor, but Novius Crispinus rose to the office of consul in 150 AD.

This man was also a Legate of the Third Legion, Legio III *'Augusta'*, in 147 AD. Historians point out that Crispinus could not have become a consul 30 years after his service in the Ninth Legion, therefore a more plausible date of his leaving would be around 130 AD – nowhere near as long ago as 119 AD!

An inscription from Misenum commemorates a soldier of the

Ninth Legion called Aelius Asclepiades. He was recruited in Cilicia and, after eight years service, died. If the inscription is genuine it would mean that the Ninth Legion was serving in the eastern part of the Empire later in Hadrian's reign.

Such evidence that a 'Ninth Legion' of some kind was in existence well after 120 AD does not discount the fact that this Legion still suffered a major defeat of some kind somewhere in the north of Britain, and that a large part of it disappeared as a result of this defeat. And it is thought, probably quite correctly, that what was left of this Ninth Legion was sent to Nijmegen in Holland to reform around the year 120 AD – but based on what evidence? It is known that the Tenth Legion (Legio X 'Gemina') held this fort from 70 AD to 104 AD; however, tiles stamped 'LEG VIIII' have been found in the ford at Nijmegen. Back in York the Legionary tiles that have been found are spelt another way: 'Leg IV HIS'.

That the Ninth Legion was at Nijmegen for some length of time is now generally accepted but when, and was it all of the Legion or just a part of it ?

In 130 AD a war against the Jews raged for about 4 or 5 years. As Fronto's letter shows (previously mentioned), heavy losses were sustained by the Romans. If the Ninth was not destroyed in this campaign, then it could equally have been the one Legion known to be destroyed by the Parthians in AD 161 – but many other Legions have also disappeared as follows:

AD 70 – 71:

Legio Ia Germanica
Legio IVa Macedonia
Legio XVa Primigenia

AD 86 – 87:

Legio Va Alavdae

AD 92:

Legio XXI Rapex

AD117 – 119? AD 132 – 135? AD 161 – 165?

Legio IX Hispana

AD 132 – 135? AD 165?

Legio XXIIa Deioteriana

Given all the evidence, the Ninth Legion could actually have disappeared in one of **three** major Roman wars: The British War, The Jewish War, or The Parthian War.

Another Legion that disappeared from the pages of history around about the same time as the later dates postulated for the Ninth was the Twenty-Second Legion, Legio XXII *'Deioteriana'*. This Legion was known to be based at Alexandria during the first century AD and thought to have disappeared somewhere between two dates, 130 AD and 165 AD, and it is recorded that yet another unnamed Legion was destroyed under Severianus in the Parthian War. That Legion is now thought to be either the XXII *'Deioteriana'* or by some the IX *'Hispana'* – the elusive Ninth Legion.

Support for this theory also comes from the fact that two new Legions were created between 130 AD and 165 AD, the II *'Italica'* and the III *'Italica'*, possibly to replace the loss of the Ninth and Twenty-Second Legions.

XIX

Author's Conclusions

Perhaps it is only right, after writing about so many possible explanations as to what might have happened to the Ninth Legion, that we put our own considered view down.

After the uprising in Britain, which happened in the north of the country, forts on the Tay were entirely cut off. The Ninth Legion was ordered by the Governor to relieve them in the spring of AD 119. It may well be that this force did reach the Tay forts. The reason we believe this is that, if the Ninth had been destroyed in the Cheviot Hills, some men would have been able to escape back to York, but evidently they did not. If we are searching for a final battle site we believe we should look to Scotland.

The Sixth Legion was sent to York to hold the north of Britain around the year 120 AD where they joined the remains of the Ninth Legion garrison left at York. However, they did not move there permanently until 124 AD. What remained of the Ninth Legion stayed on in Britain and helped in the building of Hadrian's Wall, which was built to keep out the people who had destroyed the main body of the Ninth, and all Roman forces were pulled out of Scotland behind this new fortified wall.

The Ninth Legion was then transferred to Nijmegen and built up to full strength after 124 AD under the command of Aninius Sexitus Florentinus, a man Emperor Hadrian ranked highly. By 127 AD Florentinus had been moved on after finishing the restructuring of the Legion. Three years later the Ninth Legion was hastily sent to the Jewish War around 130 AD. Here we believe it was the Ninth that suffered very heavy losses early on, and it is because of this that Hadrian decided to finally disband the 'Unlucky Ninth' for good.

We do not believe that the Legion destroyed in the Parthian War was the Ninth but rather the Twenty-Second. The remaining soldiers and officers of the Ninth were moved to other Legions or formed the basis of a new Legion, possibly the IIa *'Italica'*. At what exact date this Legion was formed is not really known except at some point well before 165 AD.

The absolute final conclusion to the Ninth Legion is that it was destroyed or disbanded between 130 AD and 135 AD due to its continuous losses and its virtual destruction in Britain in the spring or summer of 119 AD. Emperor Hadrian decided not to reform the cursed Legion and a new Legion, the IIa *'Italica'*, was probably created as a result.

But is this the 'absolute final' conclusion to the story of the Ninth Legion – or is there a sinister modern day twist to the tale still being played out?

John Aspin's Ghost Stories:

Perhaps no story, especially this one, is complete without a ghost story or two, and that is certainly true in the case of the Ninth Legion as several stories involving the Ninth are known in addition to Harry Martindale's famous encounter recorded at the beginning of this book. John Aspin was able to find this selection of some of them:

"While I was at boarding school in Scotland, at place called Rannock, there was a large moor close by called Rannoch Moor where it was said that a large force of Roman Soldiers were destroyed. This story was told to me by a friend, who was in turn told it by an old man who lived near the school. He was 84 years old and had been told it by his elderly father. The time lapse from the old man's father being told this story must be over 100 years from 1960 taking it back to the mid 1800's, to a time before widespread communication."

"Then, in a totally separate incident in the 1990's, a friend of mine

was visiting a trout farm near Rannoch while on holiday. He was told by the owner of the farm not to go out on the moor because of the swamps, workers building the railway in the last century were lost on the moor, and he then said to my friend that the Ninth Legion had also been lost somewhere out there."

These stories may well be true, for the Ninth may well have tried to campaign in Scotland after reaching the Tay forts and been cut off and lost on the moors. This would give a very good explanation why they disappeared, but this is not the only moorland legend connected to the Ninth:

"Near the town of Glossop in Derbyshire the mysterious 'Longendale Lights' are often seen eerily floating out on the moors. No one knew what these were until, so the story goes, a group of campers were lost on the moor. Being forced to pitch camp during the night they were woken by noises and saw lights heading towards them. Thinking it was a rescue party they made ready to leave but, as the lights got nearer, it became obvious they were men holding flaming torches. The leader of the group was on horseback on a large heavy horse about 15 hands high and had a plumed helmet and bronze armour breastplate. He was followed by a man carrying a standard with an eagle on it and then came soldiers carrying the torches. All were Roman soldiers of the first century AD. They past the campers without even noticing them and just carried on across the moors being watched for some time until they disappeared over a hill. The next morning the campers were found cold and shaken but all told the exact same story."

Who were these Roman soldiers? A trip to Glossop Library came up with an interesting possible explanation. The Roman General and Governor of Britain Julius Agricola (78 AD to 84 AD) is known to have been involved in heavy fighting in the Glossop area. It is also known that some units of the Ninth Legion helped in this fighting under Agricola's command. Could the Roman ghosts have been the Ninth Legion returning to the site of a previous conflict?

MARK OLLY'S GHOST STORIES:

The final ghost story connected to the Ninth Legion is probably the most famous Roman ghost story in Europe and takes us back to where we first entered this mystery. An alternative account furnishes us with the following details:

"In 1953 central heating was being installed in the Treasurer's House in York. During the installation an apprentice plumber called Harry Martindale was working down in the cellars, standing on a small ladder laying pipes, when he heard a single blast from a horn. Thinking it was traffic up above he carried on; then he heard it again but this time it came through the walls. Several times he heard the burst and each time it became louder, then suddenly a figure emerged from the wall."

"Harry, shocked, fell from the ladder to the ground. Then he saw the figure was a Roman soldier followed by another on a large shaggy horse; then, behind him, came more soldiers walking in group formation side by side. All these men looked worn out and dishevelled; they all had plume feathers in their helmets and also round shields painted green. All had dirty green cloaks around them, each carried a short sword, and all were dragging their spears along the ground. He saw about 20 Roman soldiers in total. He could now hear the horses' hooves and the soldiers murmuring to each other as they carried on through the opposite wall. One thing Harry did see was that the soldiers were not visible from below the knee."

"Harry ran for safety to the laundry above terrified. He was found a little later by the curator in a very shocked state but the curator knew what he had seen for he had also seen them before, and so had others

going back throughout the years."

When Harry made enquiries it transpired that others had also encountered the ghosts:

"In the early years of the twentieth century, a female guest of the former owner Frank Green had found her way down to the cellars blocked by a Roman soldier carrying a spear during a fancy dress party. She had motioned to go forward and the soldier had responded quite threateningly so she reported the incident. She was informed that no one had attended dressed as a Roman soldier, and this she verified for herself."

"An American professor had seen the soldiers in the 1930's, another curator had seen them in 1946 and a female curator more recently while in the cellars checking the old boiler."

Harry was questioned about what he had seen by scholars and historians and all were impressed by his accurate description. One thing, however, did appear to be new for at the time it was not thought that the Roman soldiers had round shields during the first and second century AD, but later it was discovered that Roman auxiliaries did indeed and that these 'ghost soldiers' described by Harry Martindale were, in fact, Auxiliaries of the same period as the disappearance of the Ninth Legion. Also the fact that they were not visible from the knee down was thought to be due to them standing on the Roman road of the time which led up to the headquarters, and this was evidently where the Auxiliaries were heading.

The historians who questioned Harry Martindale were in no doubt that these 'ghost soldiers' were the remains of the defeated Ninth Legion.

XX

THE LAST WORD – GHOSTS, GLADIATORS & GRAFFITI

At the time of publication Harry Martindale is in advanced old age and has been questioned many times over his sighting of the ghosts. As shown by the two accounts given in this book he has always stuck rigidly to his story – but archaeological evidence has a habit of moving on.

Recent reappraisal of his account, taking into consideration all the details he has given down the years, may now point to a date for the Auxiliaries somewhere in the third or fourth century AD and not the first century as was once thought. This would make this band of dishevelled conscripts part of the Sixth Legion and not the Ninth, possibly defeated around the time Hadrian's Wall was badly damaged by the Picts from Scotland, possibly as late as 367 AD. They would have been ready to pull out of Britain all together as the Romans did between 383 AD and 428 AD. By 414 AD Britain was left to *"look to its own defence"* and the Roman Empire here was over.

Then there's this recent discovery to consider, found by fell walkers: *"On a remote piece of moorland on the boundary between West Yorkshire and Lancashire, the Heptonstall-Thursden road crosses the Birkin Clough. Here, beside the road, an old cross is incised into a boulder but, if you set off upstream about 150 yards, there is another stone overhanging the stream. It has a flat vertical face on which some ancient graffiti artist has scratched the barely legible inscription which, at first glance, looks like 'SPCK' but, on closer examination, more likely reads 'SPQR IX'."*

Was this actually the route of the lost Ninth Legion as it marched to its final battle?

Over the past decade or so, human remains have been turning up in the gardens of houses along Driffield Terrace just outside York to the south-west, along the A1036 Tadcaster Road.

Since 2004 a concerted effort has been made by the York Archaeological Trust to excavate and identify these remains – and they have recently proved to be more than a little shocking. They appear to be Gladiators!

Reports have included such details as: *"Some of the 80 skeletal remains have been decapitated by a heavy bladed weapon of some kind, some have potential hammer blows to the head, one has been bitten by a large*  *predator such as a lion, tiger, or bear, another has his ankles in heavy iron shackles. 14 bodies so far excavated have grave goods including*  *joints of meat for the 'afterlife'. Most are individually buried tall and well-built males with well-developed fighting arms showing that they trained from youth. Some have been buried in structured graves made from stones (one in an oval shape), or* had their heads placed between their knees as is customary elsewhere in Roman burials."

From our point of view these discoveries are significant for several reasons. They span the whole occupation period of the Roman Army, from the 1st century with the Ninth Legion, right through to the 4th century under the Sixth Legion. Some of these deaths were almost certainly witnessed by the Ninth Legion and surrounding Roman Citizens. They represent the only dedicated 'Gladiator Cemetery' to survive in the Roman world so far discovered, and obviously suggest that an amphitheatre or similar arena once lay south or south-west of the city of York, probably not too far from the burial ground.

One wonders what relationship existed between these 1st and 2nd century burials and the occupation of the Ninth Legion? What nationality were these Gladiators? Did these barbaric 'games' contribute to the rebellion which eventually brought about the end of the Ninth Legion?

York Archaeological Trust continues to excavate in the City at every possible opportunity. Roman remains have recently been found in excavations in the Garden Place area off Stonebrow, just by the course of the now missing south-east Roman fort wall, along with more of the customary Viking domestic remains that have made York so internationally famous.

The final word on this, one of the world's oldest military mysteries, must be that the answer to what happened to the Ninth Legion probably still lies somewhere under the streets of modern day York, that great city founded by the Ninth Legion in AD 71 which they named 'Eboracum', a stone maybe with an inscription on it, some great archaeological discovery yet to be made, or some other lost records of the past.

Or perhaps this great and ancient City is permanently hiding the secret of the disappearing Ninth Legion beneath its pavements, never to be found?

THE END

BOOKS

O is a symbol of the world, of oneness and unity. In different cultures it also means the "eye," symbolizing knowledge and insight. We aim to publish books that are accessible, constructive and that challenge accepted opinion, both that of academia and the "moral majority."

Our books are available in all good English language bookstores worldwide. If you don't see the book on the shelves ask the bookstore to order it for you, quoting the ISBN number and title. Alternatively you can order online (all major online retail sites carry our titles) or contact the distributor in the relevant country, listed on the copyright page.

See our website **www.o-books.net** for a full list of over 500 titles, growing by 100 a year.

And tune in to myspiritradio.com for our book review radio show, hosted by June-Elleni Laine, where you can listen to the authors discussing their books.

MySpiritRadio